T. McLemore
12-23-10

Other Books by Thom S. Rainer:

Evangelism in the Twenty-first Century (editor)
The Book of Church Growth: History, Theology, and Principles
Eating the Elephant
Giant Awakenings
Effective Evangelistic Churches

America's Second Largest Generation

What They Believe.

How To Reach Them.

Bridger
THE
GENERATION

Thom S. Rainer

BROADMAN
& HOLMAN
PUBLISHERS

Nashville, Tennessee

4262-96
0-8054-6296-1

Published by Broadman & Holman Publishers, Nashville, Tennessee
Acquisitions and Development Editor: John Landers

Dewey Decimal Classification: 305.2
Subject Heading: AGE / SOCIAL GROUPS
Library of Congress Card Catalog Number: 97-11963

Unless otherwise stated all Scripture citation is from the Holy Bible, New International Version, copyright © 1973, 1978, 1984 by International Bible Society.

Library of Congress Cataloging-in-Publication Data
Rainer, Thom S.
    The bridger generation / Thom S. Rainer.
        p.   cm.
    ISBN 0-8054-6296-1 (pbk.)
    1. Children–Religious life. 2. Teenagers–Religious life. 3. Twenty-first century–Forecasts. 4. United States—Civilization—1970-   I. Title.
BV4571.2.R35   1997
261.8'3423—dc21   97–11963
                                                                              CIP

97 98 99 00 01 5 4 3 2 1

To

My three bridger sons
Sam Rainer (1980)
Art Rainer (1982)
Jess Rainer (1985)

and

Nellie Jo Rainer,
their mother and my wife,
who shaped their godly character

and in memory of

David Brown
1982–96
a bridger now with Jesus

THOM S. RAINER is the founding dean of the Billy Graham School of Missions, Evangelism, and Church Growth at The Southern Baptist Theological Seminary in Louisville, Kentucky. He is the author of six books and numerous other publications. Dr. Rainer holds the Ph.D. in evangelism from Southern Seminary and speaks in conferences, churches, and seminars throughout the U.S. each year. He is married to Nellie Jo, and they have three bridger sons: Sam, Art, and Jess.

CONTENTS

PREFACE

Welcome to the world of the bridgers, a generation of seventy-two million people born in the years 1977 to 1994. They are the second largest generation in America's history, only slightly smaller than the often-discussed baby boomers. They are the *bridge* to the next century and the next millennium, although we are not certain what kind of bridge they will be.

Several factors led me to write this book about the bridger generation. My prior books have been about the church and its evangelistic growth, so writing a generational book is a new venture for me. My first inclination to research this generation occurred in the course of nearly one hundred conferences and seminars I led over a two-year period. In these conferences I surveyed the audiences to find out when they became a Christian. To my surprise, out of the thousands surveyed, four out of five said they became a Christian during childhood or adolescence. The research led me to realize that the church cannot afford to wait for kids to reach adulthood before we evangelize them. As other Christian researchers have noted, the statistical probability of someone accepting Christ after age nineteen decreases dramatically.

A second reason for doing the research that led to this book is the sheer size of the bridger generation. The seventy-two million who comprise this generation are nearly the same size as the boomers, who were born in the years 1946 to 1964.

We need to acknowledge that the beginning point of this generation is seen differently by different experts. The issue is really when the buster generation or (generation X) *ended,* for the end of the buster generation is the beginning of the bridger generation.

Karen Ritchie, author of *Marketing to Generation X,* takes the buster generation all the way to 1981. At least two other authorities agree with her: William Strauss, author of *Generations,* and Richard Thau, executive director of the Third Millennium.

If we are to be consistent, however, with the way we defined previous generations, we must end the buster generation at 1976 and begin the bridger generation at 1977. The baby boomer generation is generally agreed to have birth dates between 1946 and 1964. These dates reflect an upsurge in live births per year, a baby boom if you will. But a new boom occurred in 1977 and continued through 1994. These are the years the bridgers were born. My perspective has the support of Diane Crispell, executive director of *American Demographics*, and Ann Clurman, partner with Yankelovich Partners.

A final reason for my interest in the bridgers is that I am the father of three bridger boys. I love my boys and I love their friends. Hardly a day goes by that the Rainer home is not filled with bridgers. My heart goes out to these kids. I pray for the best for them in this life and, more importantly, in their eternal lives.

To my knowledge, no other book has been written on this generation. And the name *bridgers* is one I originated in 1995. So, in many ways, this book will be plowing new ground.

Thanks for joining me on this journey. Visiting this generation can be a bit painful and depressing at times. They do have a lot of problems. But our God is in control. I rest my hope in His hand that we might reach the bridger generation for Christ.

ACKNOWLEDGMENTS

In February of 1980 I watched the miracle of the birth of my first child take place. As I held Sam in my arms for the first time, I was overwhelmed to the point of tears. What a blessing God had given me! Two other times I would receive that same blessing: the birth of Art in 1982 and the birth of Jess in 1985.

Little did I know that my wife and I were contributing three members to the second-largest generation in America's history. The blessings my three sons have given me are beyond description. I have been an average father at best, but they have been extraordinary sons. Thank you, guys, for loving me unconditionally. And thank you for being my inspiration to write this book.

I cannot express adequate gratitude to Sherrie Drake, my secretary, and to Chuck Lawless, my assistant. These two coworkers have put innumerable hours into this book. They have worked late hours without complaint. Sherrie and Chuck: you are a blessing to me and the Graham School team.

Thank you as well to Steve Drake. Not only has he selflessly let his wife Sherrie work these late hours; he has helped in several of the technical aspects of preparing this book. Thanks, Steve—you are always the friend who encourages and cares.

My appreciation also goes to the Broadman & Holman team, especially my editor John Landers. This book is my fifth with B & H. I am grateful to God for our partnership.

As I write these words, the book is complete, and I am sitting in my study the day after Thanksgiving Day. During this season of grateful memories, I was once again reminded of the incomparable blessing I have in my wife Jo. No man could ask for such a gift of love, patience, grace, and beauty. Our three sons are growing up to be such fine young men, Jo. I am afraid their dad had little to do with their characters. But a beautiful woman named Nellie Jo Rainer dedicated her life to raising three boys. She sacrificed a successful career for them. She gave them unconditional love. She set an example of grace and dignity which they carry to this day. And she introduced them to the Savior whom they would one day receive.

When people compliment our boys for being the fine young men they are, I am often asked "how we did it." In all honesty, I have to say that the answer is not *we* but *she*. You, Nellie Jo Rainer, have made a difference in the bridger generation because of your sacrificial love for our three bridger boys. I thank God for you. And for always, I love you.

INTRODUCTION:
WHO ARE THE BRIDGERS?

Highlights

- The bridger generation was born between 1977 and 1994.
- There are seventy-two million bridgers, the second largest generation in America's history.
- The bridgers come from a different world than previous generations in terms of race, families, economy, and religion.

The scene at the dinner table is unusual. Nothing strange or extraordinary is taking place during this meal time, but the moment is still unusual. For the first time in four months, all four members of the Turner/Johnson family are having a meal together. Life has been just too hectic, but for a moment, the Turners and Johnsons are together.

The rarity of the scene is underscored by the awkward silence at the table. Eddie Turner feels compelled to break the silence. After all, he is the husband and father—well, stepfather. His words are directed at his stepdaughter: "How was school today, Amy?"

Amy Johnson was born in 1980. The world she knows is significantly different than that of her boomer stepfather. Eddie Turner grew up in a two-parent home with a mother who stayed at home the first twelve years of his life. Both of his parents are still living and approaching nearly fifty years of marriage.

But Amy Johnson has already experienced three distinct phases of her life. For her first seven years, years that are now somewhat vague, her biological father lived at home. Then came the divorce and six years of struggle as Amy's mother barely paid the bills for the essential items of life. Though her mom's marriage to Eddie has helped make life financially easier, Amy's own perspective on life has been largely shaped by the insecurity of finances, fatherlessness, and failures.

So how should she answer her stepfather? Should she tell him that the day was miserable because of the latest boyfriend breakup? Should she express her general distrust of males because they always leave? Should she tell him that she daydreamed during Algebra II class, wondering how she would make it financially when she finally (if ever) is on her own? "No, he would not understand," she concludes. Her response is a non-enthusiastic and less-than-credible "fine."

The attention turns to Michael Johnson. Michael was born in 1983 and has even fewer memories than Amy of his biological father being home. He cannot understand why his stepfather insisted they have a meal together. After all, the Turner/Johnson family usually eats on the run with little regard for time together as a family. And Michael resents Eddie's intrusion into his early evening enjoyment of MTV. Would this meal time ever end?

Michael is not about to tell either his mother or his stepfather about the preoccupation of his mind. When he began seeing Lisa, their relationship proceeded from casual to intimate rather quickly. He is not that concerned about Lisa becoming pregnant; he could find the money for an abortion. But Michael heard just yesterday of a college friend who tested HIV positive. And the speaker at school reminded the students once again that his age group is the segment of the population with the fastest increase in the number of AIDS cases. Michael just wants the meal to end so he can get on the Internet and forget his worries for a while.

Four people at the table from two very different worlds. Eddie and Sue Turner: boomer parents struggling to keep a second marriage intact and two children/stepchildren happy. Amy and Michael Johnson: two bridger young people with worries and problems their parents/stepparents never knew.

Meet the Bridgers

Amy and Michael belong to a generation that will, in many ways, define the twenty-first century for America. They and their peers were born between 1977 and 1994 and account for seventy-two million of the nation's population. The bridgers are only slightly smaller than the baby boomers whose population reached seventy-six million. But the influence of the bridgers could be greater.

This generation has been unnamed for the most part. In isolated articles some writers have referred to them as "the next boom," "the echo-boomers," "the new boom," "the vava boom" (because so many of the mothers of this generation had their first child later in life, usually in their thirties), and "the millennial generation."

I have named this generation "the bridgers" for three reasons. First and foremost, these seventy-two million will *bridge* two centuries and two millennia. Though their birth dates will have twentieth-century markings, their influence will be felt strongest as they enter adulthood in the twenty-first century.

A second reason for using the bridger nomenclature is one of hope and promise. While we are living in a time of upheaval and uncertainty, we are also paradoxically living in a time of unprecedented awakenings, prayer movements, and awareness of God. Indeed, the bridger generation is already being cited as a "religious" generation, though "religious" and "Christian" are hardly synonymous. But is it possible that this group of seventy-two million may be the *bridge* between the secular and the sacred?

A third motive behind the bridger terminology is one of practicality and alliteration. Previous generations have been dubbed "builders," "boomers," and "busters." "Bridgers" is a neat addition to the generations family of "b's."

Before we examine in detail the bridgers, let us take a cursory look at the preceding generations. Perhaps the most notable aspects of the predecessor generations are the stark contrasts they provide when compared to the bridgers.

The Generations Before

Depending upon which demographer you trust, America has anywhere from four to six generations alive today. I will present four generations, with the recognition that the oldest of the groups could easily be two distinct generations.

The Builders (Born 1910–46)

Chart 1 shows that the builders were a fairly stable generation in terms of annual births. The number of births in the United States each year during this period remained fairly steady, around 2.5 to 3.0 million births per year.

The older portion of this generation, born before 1933, is often called the World War II or "GI generation" since many of its members fought in the war. Two significant events shaped the values and attitudes of the GI generation: the war and the Great Depression. This generation has been

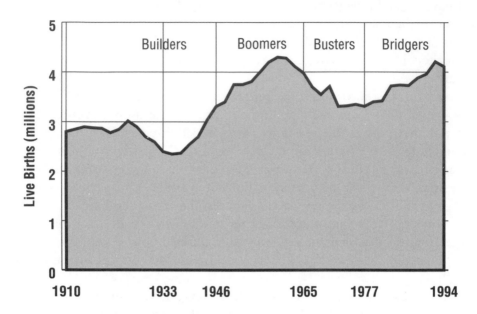

Chart 1
A Century of Booms and Busts

one of the most powerful groups our nation has known. They are the first full generation to enjoy the benefits of Social Security, yet their affluence would be noticeable even without Social Security.

The World War II generation will be remembered as an affluent elderly group. They benefited from an expanding economy, rising real estate values, and generous government programs. Interestingly, their wealth has not been dependent upon lengthy education. A high-school education was sufficient to find a good-paying, secure job in their early adult years. This lower level of education engenders different perspectives compared to boomers, busters, and bridgers.

The younger portion of the builder generation was born between 1933 and 1945. One of the earlier names given to this relatively small group was the "silent generation" because few of its members held high-profile business or political positions (for example, no United States president has come from this generation). However, few demographers call them the silent generation today. Members of this group now head most of the nation's corporations, and many are in positions of governmental and political leadership.

This portion of the builder generation is now more commonly known as the "swing generation." The thirty million persons born between 1933 and

1945 find themselves caught between two potent and influential generations, the World War II generation and the boomers. Some of the generation swing toward the more casual lifestyle commonplace with many boomers; others swing to the conservative views of their World War II elders.

While the swing generation's small size (only 11.7 percent of the United States population in 1995) may give the appearance of having little influence, theirs has actually been the generation that experienced the greatest level of affluence. Competition for first entry level, then middle management, and then upper management positions was not as intense for the swing generation. Their small number meant a relatively low supply of persons to fill a relatively high demand for employees. One demographer has suggested that, with the present economic scenario, their group "may be the last generation to enjoy affluence in their retirement years."[1]

The Boomers

Baby boomers were born between 1946 and 1964. This largest generation in America's history is the most-discussed, most-marketed, and most-debated generation ever. Their sheer size has caught the attention of business, schools, the media, and churches for the past four decades. "Whatever the baby boom does becomes the 'in' thing to do, from wearing bell-bottoms to buying minivans. . . . The nation has had to put up with the overwhelming demands for housing and jobs, and eventually it will have to cope with the boomers' demands for Social Security benefits."[2]

The majority of the boomers were raised by stay-at-home mothers who were younger than the mothers of today. They are the Woodstock and Vietnam generation that believed their way was *the* way. In the 1960s the boomers were counter-cultural and anti-authoritarian. That self-centered independent spirit became a self-centered materialistic spirit in the 1980s. But in the decade of the nineties, the energy of the boomers became apparent in the growth of New Age spiritualism and the self-help movement.

In 1995, the boomers accounted for 29.5 percent of the total population of the United States. The contrast of the size of the boomers to the busters, for example, is stark: seventy-two million versus forty-four million.

No generation in history had its own generational literary genre until the boomers. At least thirty books on baby boomers have been written from a Christian perspective. Well over one hundred secular writings have been added to the boomer-topic library.

The Busters

The buster label remains with those born between 1965 and 1976, despite attempts by some to shed the less-than-positive description. The bust, of course, is the dramatic downturn in the number of annual births after the explosive baby boom of 1946 to 1964. In 1965, the first year of the baby bust, births dropped below 3.8 million. The downturn continued until 1976, when only 3.2 million babies were born.

"Generation X" is the nomenclature of choice of this post-boomer group. But even this label came from a nondescript novel by Douglas Coupland. And a 1995 MTV poll found that only one in ten persons in this generation accepts the Generation X label.[3] Most of these young adults prefer no label at all. Said rapper Dr. Dre, born in 1966: "I haven't heard anyone in my 'hood' talking about it. The only X I know is Malcom X."[4]

The busters are sometimes called slackers, but the critics are typically condescending boomers. The busters are no less diligent than any previous generation in their young adulthood, especially the boomers.

The busters are stereotyped as pessimists, perhaps with some justification. From an economic viewpoint, Generation X entered the job market during difficult times. It is hardly surprising that they are both cautious and pessimistic about their long-term financial prospects.

And Now—The Bridgers

If Americans have had an unusual fascination with the large boomer population, just wait until the bridgers become adult consumers. Chart 2 shows how closely the two huge population groups compare. The first baby boom was one year longer and four million larger than this second boom we have named the bridgers. Still the parallels between the two generations are remarkable.

In the twenty-first century the bridgers will shape the attitudes, values, economics, and lifestyles of America. They will be the dominant adult population group for at least the first half of the next century. In 1995, the bridgers accounted for 27.5 percent of the total United States population. Though the boomers were slightly larger, the bridgers will be the ones moving into positions of power and influence in the twenty-first century.

Chart 2
Two Baby Booms and How They Grew

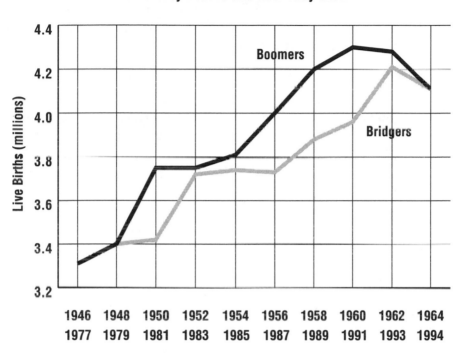

The Bridger's Share of the U.S. Population, 1995

	Number (thousands)	% of Total Population
Total (all age groups)	262,754	100.0
Bridgers (1977–94)	72,176	27.5
Busters (1965–76)	44,603	17.0
Boomers (1946–64)	77,587*	29.5
Builders (before 1946):		
Swing (1933–45)	30,728	11.7
World War II (before 1933)	37,662	14.3

* The boomers are typically numbered at 76 million, which represents the number of live births in the U.S. for this generation. This higher number of over 77 million takes into account immigrants who were not born in the U.S.

Source: Bureau of the Census, Projections of the United States by Age, Sex, Race, and Hispanic Origin: 1992 to 2050. Due to rounding, the figures in the "number (thousands)" column do not add precisely.

The bridgers will not fit the molds nor the expectations of the boomers, whose condescending attitudes toward other generations will be challenged by a group that will refuse to be stereotyped. Just look at the different cultural characteristics of the two largest generations in order to sense the significant perspectives of the boomers and the bridgers.

Two Different Worlds

Boomers	Bridgers
Cold War	regional wars
nuclear threat	terrorist threats
economic prosperity	economic uncertainty
mother's care	day care
"Father Knows Best"	Father isn't home
TV dinners	low-fat fast food
network TV	cable TV
45s and "American Bandstand"	CDs and MTV
Ma Bell	Internet
VW buses	minivans and SUVs
Free love	condoms
VD	AIDS
monocultural	multicultural

Source: *American Demographics* (some are original with author)

The bridgers are also a much more confident and ambitious generation than the boomers. We can make that assessment at least with the older bridgers. Look at the attitudes of college freshmen in 1971 (boomers) and 1993 (older bridgers):

Attitudes of College Freshmen
1971 (boomers) and 1993 (bridgers)

Reasons noted as very important in deciding to go to college:

	Boomers 1971	Bridgers 1993
parents wanted me to go	22.9%	34.6%
get a better job	73.8%	82.1%
gain general education	59.5%	65.3%
make more money	49.9%	75.1%
learn more about things	68.8%	75.2%
prepare for graduate/professional school	34.5%	61.2%

Objectives considered to be essential or very important:

	Boomers 1971	Bridgers 1993
raise a family	60.2%	70.6%
be very well off financially	40.1%	74.5%
help others in difficulty	62.7%	63.3%
be successful in own business	41.9%	42.6%
participate in community action	25.9%	25.6%

Students who rated themselves above average in:

	Boomers 1971	Bridgers 1993
academic ability	50.6%	56.2%
leadership ability	34.9%	55.9%
mathematical ability	32.0%	43.0%
popularity	29.2%	45.6%
self-confidence (intellectual)	34.8%	59.6%
self-confidence (social)	27.4%	51.3%

Source: *The American Freshman*, Higher Education Research Institute, University of California-Los Angeles.

Again the contrasts between the two generations are amazing. The bridgers in much greater numbers than the boomers go to college for a better job, for a better education, and to make more money. While only one-third of the boomer freshmen in 1971 considered graduate or professional school a good option, over 60 percent of the bridgers have ambitions for post-baccalaureate education.

The bridgers are more confident than the boomer freshmen in their academic ability, leadership ability, mathematical ability, popularity, and social skills. But they are no less likely to be altruistic in helping others and participating in community service. And lest one thinks family values are diminishing in importance, over 70 percent of the bridger freshmen consider raising a family to be essential or very important. Only 60 percent of the boomer freshmen felt this way in 1971.

In this book we will examine numerous characteristics and facets of the bridger generation. We will look at their attitudes, family background, racial and cultural concerns, economic worries, media preoccupations, fears, and faiths. We will look at a generation raised in a time when a nation is questioning its own values and priorities. And we will look at a group of seventy-two million young people who may very well be the most promising generation our nation has ever known.

But the promise and hope that we have for the bridger generation is not certain. Though they may have high career and family expectations, the bridgers are totally confused about matters of faith and absolutes. And we who are in the boomer generation are largely to blame. Many of our peers, through their words, actions, or both, communicated to their children that matters of faith were optional at best and unimportant at worst. We raised a generation that knows not absolutes, Scripture, or the exclusivity of salvation through Jesus Christ.

While this book is in general terms about a generation in its demographic realities, it is first a book written by a Christian who believes that there is no other name by which people can be saved except that of Jesus Christ (Acts 4:12). It is a book that looks at a generation objectively in statistical terms, but one that exudes a passion to reach that generation for Christ.

The person, therefore, who does not consider himself or herself to be a follower of Christ should find a plethora of information in this book about America's second largest generation. But I approach this work with an unapologetic belief in Christ and the exclusivity of salvation through Him. I researched and wrote this book first as a Christian seeking to obey the Great Commission (Matt. 28:18–20). The demographic and statistical research was incidental to this primary purpose.

Where does the church begin, therefore, with its desire to reach the bridgers? Perhaps a good starting point is understanding the generation. That is the reason this book was written. It is my prayer that you will indeed have a better understanding of the bridgers when you finish reading this book. Before we proceed further, though, allow me to introduce you to some of the major characteristics of the bridgers.

The World of the Bridgers

What are the shaping influences on the bridger generation? Though we will answer this question in greater detail in subsequent chapters, some general comments are needed to introduce this huge generation of Americans.

Their Multiracial World

The boomers grew up in a multiracial nation that was largely segregated. While some of the boomers attended integrated schools, their social world was largely segregated. The bridgers, however, know that their world is both multiracial and multicultural.

Three-fourths of the boomers are non-Hispanic white. Only 67 percent of the bridgers are non-Hispanic white. By 1994, only 64 percent of the infants born fit this racial classification. Very few of the baby boom generation are mixed-race persons. But, among the bridgers, nearly two million have been born to parents of different races.

The aggressive world of consumer marketing already recognizes the significant level of diversity among the children who are today's bridgers: "One reflection of racial and ethnic diversity among children can be seen in the toy market. Mattel, Tyco Toys, and Playskool are just some of the big players that are responding to ethnic and racial diversity."[5] One toy company executive explains: "We have Dream Doll House families that are African-American, Hispanic, Asian, and Caucasian," says Laurie Strong of Fisher-Price, a subsidiary of Mattel.[6]

The increased diversity is engendering two significantly different responses from the bridgers. On the one hand, a sizable number of bridgers are calling for greater tolerance. A majority of the bridgers ages twelve to seventeen believe members of minority racial and ethnic groups receive too little respect.[7]

On the other hand, not all school integration has been successful. Many neighborhoods and schools are as segregated as ever. Race-related violence is increasing, and reports of racial hate groups appear regularly. Many schools around the United States report increasing racial tension among their students.

The bridgers of the twenty-first century may very well be the generation of paradox in racial issues. Among the seventy-two million persons in this generation, we will likely find the greatest level of racial tolerance our nation has ever known *and* the most intense bigotry a generation has produced in a century.

Their Diverse Families

Susan Mitchell suggests the introductory question of children boomers was: "What does your father do for a living?" But, she proposes, the question of children bridgers is: "Does your dad live with you?"[8] The following statistics show the dramatic change in families from the 1970 boomers to the 1993 bridgers:

	Children Boomers 1970	Children Bridgers 1993
Two-parent homes-all	85%	71%
Two-parent homes-black	64%	39%*
Two-parent homes-white	90%	77%*
One-parent homes-all	12%	27%
One-parent homes-black	35%	60%*
One-parent homes-white	10%	22%*
Living with a never-married-mother—all	7%	31%*

* 1990 statistics

Only 71 percent of the bridgers are living with two parents at home. The African-American population has an even higher incidence of one-parent homes. Six out of ten African-American bridgers live with only one parent, usually the mother.

By the twenty-first century, fewer than one-half of the bridgers may have spent their childhood with both biological parents. The social, financial, and psychological impact of the new bridger families will be factors considered in chapters 2 and 3.

One positive statement that can be made about bridger families is that the generation gap between parents and children is virtually nonexistent. The boomers and their parents experienced a tremendous chasm as a result of their conflicting values. Interestingly, the boomers are still experiencing a generation gap with their parents, even though the older boomers have passed their fiftieth birthday. Many demographers claim that the gap persists because of the higher educational attainment of the boomers compared to that of their less-educated builder parents.[9]

But the education gap between the bridgers and their parents will be negligible. Many of the boomers' parents did not complete high school, but almost 90 percent of the boomers did. The bridgers should experience at least the same high school graduation rate as the boomers. One-fourth of the boomers completed college; the Census Bureau projects that same level for the bridgers.[10]

The boomers are surprised to discover that their bridger children believe their parents are informed about the music they like, according to a *Good Housekeeping* and Roper Starch Worldwide study in 1993.[11] "The children surveyed also say their parents' opinions matter most to them when it comes to drinking, spending money, and questions about sex and AIDS. They even listen more to their parents than their friends about which snack foods to eat."[12]

Their Economic World

The bridger generation is already divided economically between the "haves" and "have-nots." With each consecutive year of birth from 1977 to 1994, the poverty rate increased among the bridger children. Those born in 1977 had a poverty rate of 16 percent, while the bridgers born in 1993 had a poverty rate of 23 percent. Significantly, 46 percent of the black bridger children live in poverty, compared to 18 percent of the white children. The bridgers may thus be a generation in conflict in terms of class and race.

Like their predecessor buster generation, the bridgers are not confident about the American economy in the long-term. But, unlike the busters, the bridgers have a high level of confidence that they can do well individually, even though the economy will suffer in the aggregate.

Their Religious World

Perhaps more than any twentieth-century generation, the bridgers are a religious group. But "religious" is about as specific as one can get in describing their beliefs. The bridgers as a generation believe in almost any expression of a higher being or higher power. And they resist any claim that one faith system is superior or exclusive. The church has an awesome challenge to share an exclusive gospel with a generation that resists absolutes of any type.

Much publicity has been engendered about America's preoccupation with New Age religions. But the primary "competition" for the bridgers' allegiance may come from a growing religious force in America—Muslims. A 1991 poll of twelve- to seventeen-year-olds by George H. Gallup International Institute confirmed the increasing influence of Muslims in America. Almost three-fourths of the respondents said that they receive too little information at school about Muslims.[13] They were actually asking for religious instruction in public schools, but the instruction they desired was not Christian.

The church in America has intentionally attempted to reach two earlier generations, the boomers and the busters. In terms of generational penetration, the efforts have largely been a failure. What can we learn from these earlier experiences as we try to reach the bridgers?

The Church: Learning from Past Failures

In both the boomer and the buster generations, the church did experience a season of success in reaching a large number from each group. But the success was ephemeral. The quick surge of church growth from these generations was almost equally matched by a quick exodus over three to seven years. Two primary factors explain this phenomenon in simplistic terms.

Mistake #1: Eagerness to Accommodate

Church leaders of the seventies through the nineties were told that they and their churches were hopelessly out of date and out of touch. The forms and liturgies of worship, the ancient hymns, and fifties-style buildings were irrelevant to the unchurched generations. For the most part, the critics were right. The evangelical church did not understand the culture it was trying to reach. Change was needed.

But some churches went overboard in making changes. For these churches, changes in style shifted to changes in substance. The user-friendly exuberance led to low expectations and subtle encouragement of biblical illiteracy. So the boomers and busters entered the church looking for something different. They were initially attracted by the relevancy of the worship, the ability to remain anonymous, and the hope of the Christian faith. But they quietly left the church when they discovered it to be amazingly similar to the world they knew. They were looking for something different; what they found was often more worldly than heavenly. They were looking for a challenge; what they found was the lowest of expectations.

Mistake #2: Waiting for Adulthood

A second major mistake made by many churches attempting to reach the boomers and busters is that they waited until these generations reached adulthood. But the most receptive time of a person's life to be reached for the gospel is when he or she is a teenager. Nearly 90 percent of all persons who accept Christ become Christians before they turn twenty years old.

The time to reach the bridgers is now, not the year 2010. We will discuss this issue in detail in chapter 10.

The Church and the Bridgers: A Time of Challenge—A Time of Hope

This book was written with the primary purpose of communicating ways the church can reach America's second largest generation. If one focuses upon the statistics of family breakdowns, increasing crime, decreasing commitments, and uncertain attitudes toward the church, the opportunities for reaching the bridgers may appear dismal.

But this book would not have been written unless real hope and promise were present. Despite the dire and gloomy statistics we often hear and read, something significantly positive is taking place in our nation—something that most of the media have largely ignored.

A prayer movement is renewing churches, college campuses, and denominations. Real life-changing brokenness, reconciliation, and renewal have been reported in many areas across the United States.[14] Promise Keepers has become a movement in itself. Hundreds of thousands of men gather in football stadiums in our nation each year. Many accept Christ. Others renew their commitments to their families and their Lord. The absentee father may become the godly father.

A renewed hunger for God's Word abounds. Expository preaching, a verse-by-verse unearthing of the treasures of Scripture, is the fastest-growing preaching style in evangelistic churches. Likewise, Sunday morning Bible study, still called Sunday School in many churches, is on the rebound after many pundits had predicted its demise.[15]

God has given the church in America a new opportunity to reach a generation that may be the most influential group in our nation's history. One demographer, not necessarily writing from a Christian perspective, sees that same opportunity: "As a new century begins, the next baby boom will enter the adult world and begin struggling with [their] problems. But their place in the record books is already secure. They may one day surpass their parents to become the largest and most influential generation in U.S. history."[16]

Perhaps a good biblical analogy can be found in the Old Testament promise to Joshua. The nation of Israel had been given the opportunity to enter the promised land forty years earlier. But fear and compromise superseded their trust in God and His promises. As a consequence, the people did not enter the promised land. They were sentenced to a forty-year wilderness wandering, where a whole generation died.

Forty years later, a new leader named Joshua succeeded Moses. Once again the people of Israel were given the promise that their God would be with them when they entered the promised land. They had been given a second opportunity.

Most American churches had their opportunity to reach the largest generation in American history in the sixties through the eighties. But the final assessment seems to be that the boomers will remain the largest unchurched generation in history.

But our God has given us another opportunity. A new generation, nearly as large as the boomers, waits for evangelization and ministry. We must not fail. We cannot fail. As we seek to reach the bridgers, we must ever be aware of their culture and attitudes. We must seek the most appropriate methodologies and means to reach them. But this time, more than ever, we must realize that our strength and resources cannot ultimately be our own. This time, more than ever, we must seek the face of God to reach a generation.

And like the promises given to Joshua and Israel, those same words of God return to the church today: "Be strong and very courageous. Be careful to obey all the law my servant Moses gave you; do not turn from it to the right or to the left, that you may be successful wherever you go. . . . Have I not commanded you? Be strong and courageous. Do not be terrified; do not be discouraged, for the LORD your God will be with you wherever you go" (Josh. 1:7, 9).

Welcome to the world of the bridgers. May God be with you wherever you go to reach them.

CHAPTER 1

The Minds of the Bridgers

Highlights

- The bridger generation is very worried about the education they are receiving.
- No generation at this young age has experienced more stress.
- This generation is the most serious yet.
- The bridgers could be called "the visual generation."
- The bridgers worry about money.

> *We're supposed to be stressed-out, pessimistic, lonely, and frustrated. At least that's what the media tells us. Actually, I'm basically a happy guy, and I think most of my friends are too. I sure hope my generation doesn't buy into everything we're told.*
>
> Todd, a seventeen-year-old bridger
> from Mississippi

In the next chapter you will read some gloomy statistics about the bridgers and their families. The breakdown of the family is no doubt a major concern for the second largest generation in America's history. Yet recent studies show that the bridgers are not nearly as pessimistic about themselves as older generations are about them.

In a study of older bridgers, the research found some encouraging self-portraits among the 723 bridgers interviewed:[1]

- Approximately 80 percent describe themselves as "excited about life."
- Three out of four claim they are "trusting of other people."
- Nearly 75 percent say they are "optimistic about the future."
- Two-thirds see themselves as leaders.
- Only a minority admit that they are "stressed out."
- Less than 20 percent say they are "lonely."
- Only 20 percent describe themselves as "discouraged."

Still other data indicate, however, that when pressed about specific issues, the bridgers are not as optimistic as the brief descriptive surveys indicate. Indeed, the bridgers are a generation of paradox. On the surface, they will tell you that life is fine and that their future is bright. But dig a little deeper and they will confess some deep concerns.

What is on the minds of the bridgers? What are their attitudes and out-looks? In this chapter we will attempt to hear this generation describe their feelings and perspectives. Their concerns of today will profoundly impact the nation they will lead in the twenty-first century.

What Is on Their Minds?

When we look at the major fears of the bridgers in chapter 7, we will see some of the expected topics: AIDS, crime, drugs, environmental problems, and the like. Interestingly, however, the number one issue on the minds of the bridgers is none of the above, but perhaps a surprising revelation: a good education. We will examine that issue first, followed by other attitudinal profiles of the generation.

Reading, Writing, and a Whole Lot More!

Perhaps because virtually all of the bridgers are in school now, their educa-tion is the number one topic on their minds. Yet their concern for education is more than a reflection of the life phase through which they are passing. Indeed, the boomers were far less concerned about education when they were students. As we saw in the last chapter, bridger college freshmen take more seriously their academic ability, mathematical ability, and a desire for gradu-ate education than the boomer freshmen did nearly thirty years ago.[2]

Interestingly, it is the boomer parents of the bridgers who are at least some-what responsible for the children's attitude about education. The boomers thought they could solve the world's problems just by their presence and demographic power. One boomer describes his journey from idealism to realism: "It wasn't until the 1980's that the Me Generation realized what it had been missing: a We Generation. We had spent so long defining ourselves as *not* our parents, trying on hairstyles and ideologies, being angry at *them*, that we had no identity of our own. Having children changed all that. Finally there was another generation, one that could be identified as *not us*. . . . They took our measure, and we were, as parents always are, found wanting. Our high divorce rate, our drug excesses, our preoccupation with material goods . . . we had all the fun, they got the hangover: the buster families, the shopping malls, the AIDS virus."[3]

The boomers realized that their excesses had not produced the utopia they initially believed was possible. Then they had children. Since their previous ways had failed, the new parents turned to the old-fashioned basics of success and achievement. They desired that their bridger children get the best education possible. Numerous researchers have discovered that boomer parents are often more concerned about their kids' school achievement than any other area of their lives.[4]

Bridgers are being judged today by their classroom achievements more than any other measure. So when asked what is on their mind, the largest number of bridgers responded that they desire good grades and acceptance into a good college.[5] Such concerns were expressed by bridgers in all parts of this nation and in all socioeconomic groups.

It is little wonder that bridgers who make "As" are more excited, trusting, and optimistic than "C" students, while the lower academic-performing bridgers are more stressed out, lonely, and discouraged.[6] Education preoccupies the minds of the bridgers. Such an orientation will have significant implications for our nation in the twenty-first century.

While the bridgers have education on their mind, they are less inclined to do something about it. Over three-fourths of U.S. high school seniors spend fewer than five hours a week on homework. By comparison, only 35 percent of their Japanese peers spend so little time on homework.[7]

A cursory glance at the state of American education reveals a disturbing predicament for the bridgers.

- Only a third of seniors mastered reading passages in a 1994 test by the National Assessment of Educational Progress. A mere 11 percent showed a good grasp of history. And the average reading level of black seventeen-year-olds is the same as that of white thirteen-year-olds.[8]
- In Japan, 70 percent of math classes focus on advanced concepts such as algebra, while fewer than 10 percent of the classes in the United States do so.

- Advanced placement exams in the United States ignore the topics of organic chemistry and biochemistry. In Germany, one-fourth of such exams include these subjects.
- Students in Great Britain are required to master a range of drama, fiction, and poetry, including such literary greats as Shakespeare and George Orwell. Only one-third of U.S. high school seniors have this competency.
- Among fourth grade U.S. students, only 7 percent can write a persuasive essay meeting suggested standards; 78 percent cannot meet geography standards; 80 percent cannot meet mathematics standards; and over 80 percent failed to meet history standards.
- High school students in Japan, France, and Germany spend more than twice the time in class studying math, history, and science as U.S. students do.
- The average number of days in the school year by nation is:
    Japan - 240
    Korea - 222
    Taiwan - 222
    Israel - 215
    Scotland - 191
    Canada - 188
    United States - 178[9]

The tension is obvious. The bridgers have education as the foremost issue on their mind, but the system is failing them, and they are failing the system. The generation is yielding to the temptation to spend inordinate amounts of time in other pursuits—particularly television viewing—when they could be meeting their heartfelt desire to learn.

But the system is failing as well. Some blame lack of parental involvement (some boomer parents are still in a continuous mode of self-centeredness); others blame lack of discipline; and yet some point to inadequate funding and lack of local control in schools. The reasons for the problems with the educational system may not be clearly identified, but the results are. We are producing a generation that has learned less than any generation in this century. The greater tragedy is that the bridgers seem truly desirous of education, but what we are offering them is mediocre at best and irrelevant at worst.

Stressed-out Minds

Despite Todd's rosy scenario of the stress-free bridgers at the beginning of this chapter, his generation may be the generation that has experienced the most stress in our nation's history. Once you start asking probing questions about their state of mind, you quickly learn that their lives are tense and intense.

I learned this message in one of my own son's lives recently. I like to believe that my three bridger sons have a fairly good life: good school, economic security, intact family, Christian values, etc. I never really thought that any of my boys would be stressed.

But I learned differently. Since I travel frequently, I like to take my wife and/or my three boys with me on some of my trips. On one particular journey, I took Art (born 1982) with me to Alabama where I was speaking at a Christian retreat. The flight from Louisville to Birmingham was uneventful, and the retreat center offered little for Art except sleeping, hiking, and shooting basketball.

Fearful that he would tell me that the trip was one of the most boring events of his life, I did not inquire of him as we left the retreat. But as we were leaving, Art volunteered: "Dad, you know I had a good time just doing *nothing*. For three days, I didn't have to worry about being in a hundred different places to do a hundred different things."

Art was telling me that he was simply stressed because of his schedule. Christian leaders are recognizing that even Christian youth are too busy. Richard Ross has been a youth minister for more than two decades. Early in his ministry he rarely talked with teenagers about an upcoming event more than two weeks in advance. "If I did, they would just shrug their shoulders," Ross explained. "But today, even when I talk about trips and events months in advance, a lot of the older youth start pulling out their planning notebooks or calendars to make sure they don't already have something planned."[10]

While adolescence has always been a time of surging hormones and growing independence, the bridgers have a plethora of other issues with which to deal. We seem to be expecting this young generation to skip childhood and youth and barge right into the responsibilities of adulthood.

Many of today's youth have home responsibilities that were not thrust upon previous generations until after high school. They are expected to take charge of the household while Mom and Dad are busy earning a living with multiple jobs and pursuing their own desires. It is no surprise that some have dubbed these young people "the latchkey generation." Never have so many expectations been placed on such a young group. Barna states the situation of the bridgers well: "They have not had the requisite time to explore the mysteries and snares of the world without external expectations. They have not had the opportunity to plumb the depths of their characters, to figure out who they really are, or to learn more about what is really important to them. They have been robbed of the incubation period necessary to allow their minds, bodies, and spirits to develop more fully and get in synch before dealing with the enormously complex realities of life in a civilized society at the close of the twentieth century."[11]

The stress that the bridgers feel is related to a myriad of other factors, most of which we will explore later in this book. For now, let's look at some of the factors that add stress to their lives:

- The bridgers are the first generation raised predominantly by working mothers. Neither parent has been home in daytime hours for a majority of the bridgers.
- They are growing up with the highest crime rate ever. As one demographer noted: "These children have stared at photos of stolen children every time they drank milk."[12]
- They are growing up in the most fragmented families of any American generation.
- They are confused about leaders in our nation who seem to say one thing but do another.
- Peer pressure and issues of sexuality are ever-present stress issues; AIDS looms before bridgers as the great plague (the bridgers are the segment of the population with the greatest increase in the number of AIDS cases), but every twenty-one seconds, a fifteen- to nineteen-year-old female loses her virginity.[13]

So what is on the minds of bridgers? Stress and a lot of it. At the end of this chapter we will look at some of the challenges this presents to the church.

Independence vs Dependence

A major shaping attitude of the bridgers is the issue of independence versus dependence. From the time a child learns to walk, he or she is always pushing his or her parents for more independence. With past generations (perhaps the boomers excluded), parents have granted increasing independence gradually and incrementally. Though children have outwardly cried out for greater freedom, inwardly they desire boundaries, standards, and even rules. The majority of the bridgers have known none of these.

Mike is a fourteen-year-old from Georgia. His peers envy him because his parents treat him as an adult. "They tell me that I can make my own decisions and live with them. They don't set a time when I have to be home at night. And I don't have my driver's license, so I hang out with kids a lot older than me."

The other teenage bridgers in the focus group are shaking their heads. One boy expresses the sentiments of some of the others: "Man, you're lucky. My parents are always on my case. 'Be home by ten!' they tell me. I wish I had your parents."

The group is quiet for a moment. With uncertainty Mike speaks softly. "You guys don't understand. I really want my parents to give me some rules. Sometimes I wonder if they really care about me at all."[14]

Because adulthood has been forced upon the bridgers prematurely, they are far more independent than previous generations in several areas. For example, the latchkey generation appears better equipped to care for themselves and their siblings, but this same generation is less communicative. This greater independence "also fosters that aloofness and distancing that is a sign of stress [which] has become more common with children."[15]

The bridgers' increased independence has meant that they have the freedom to acquire more information earlier through various media, particularly television. The free-flowing availability of information has certainly made them more savvy about the ways of the world, but it also has tended to make them more pessimistic and less idealistic.

Early indications tell us that the opening of the door to greater opportunities for independence may have negative consequences as the bridgers enter adulthood. The bridgers are more insecure about forming relationships or dealing with anyone outside the security of their own home.[16] Arguably, factors other than early independence may have contributed to this attitude. But the most recent research indicates that missing out on childhood may have detrimental effects in adulthood.

Paradoxically, the generation that assumed household responsibilities at the earliest age may also be the generation that leaves that home at the latest age. Such was the trend for their predecessor generation, the busters, but the busters stayed at home longer primarily for economic reasons. The bridgers may remain at home even longer, but more for reasons of emotional insecurity than economic uncertainty.

A Very Serious Group of People!

Carefree childhoods are not the norm for the majority of the bridgers. While older generations had the opportunity to experience "the dreamy imagination [which] many think is a key to a satisfactory adulthood,"[17] the bridgers "face much more serious problems than the boomers did when they were children. AIDS, crime, violence, and divorce cast long shadows over their world. As the children of working parents, they often have to assume adult responsibilities at an early age."[18]

Our data on the older bridgers indicate that they already are thinking about matters of seriousness more commonly identified with young adults in their mid and late twenties. They are focusing on the best way to get a better job, a better education, a better financial position, and better leadership skills.[19] And remember, these are teenagers who are pondering such serious matters!

One does not have to speak with bridgers long to sense the deep and pensive attitudes of these young people. In one focus group in Georgia, the older bridgers spent approximately three-fourths of their conversation talking about matters that were once the domain of adulthood. I listened to thirteen- and fourteen-year-olds express fears about violence, the economy, and their families. And I heard them making plans for adulthood that I did not even consider until I entered college.

Some of the over-seriousness of the bridgers reflects the adult choices this group has made. But much of their solemnity stems from the expectations placed upon them by the adults in their worlds.

Parents want their children to adhere to a value system but give them no absolutes to which to turn. Schools are warned not to communicate values, and many churches also have failed to communicate a coherent value system. Today's adults cry in anguish because today's youth show little concern for matters of right and morality. But only a minority of the adults could point a bridger to a set of values and tell him or her where to find right and wrong.

Adults of today know that the rise of teenage pregnancies harms individuals and society at large. But why should we be surprised that kids are having kids? We allow the world of sex-without-boundaries to enter their minds through a barrage of media instruments. Indeed, the adults are the ones who are creating such messages.

We adults also are sending mixed messages on the matters of character and integrity. We tell the bridgers that character is important, but we no longer hold our nation's leadership accountable for character. We tell them that effective leadership is the key issue, regardless of character, as if the two can be separated.

Is it any wonder then that these young people born between 1977 and 1994 are perhaps the most serious children and adolescents in our nation's history? Childhood is to be a time of play and fun. Have we robbed our children of their laughter?

The Visual Generation

One way to know what is on the minds of the bridgers is to see what they are watching. More than any previous generation, theirs is characterized by the statement, "I saw, therefore I am." One demographer explains: "They can take in and sort through visual information to a remarkable degree. They appreciate the subtleties of media presentations—from a well-made special effect in a movie to an effective concept in a music video. They are comfortable with technology—really the first generation ever to be so. Don't underestimate the eventual impact of this characteristic."[20]

In chapter 6 we will explore in-depth this "media generation." For now let us see how the visual world affects the minds and dispositions of the bridgers.

Visually Sophisticated. The bridgers "are able to take in information visually as never before, and they are adept at visual interrelationships of objects and images."[21] If you are a buster, boomer, or a builder, I challenge you to a test case with a bridger. Rent a movie video and watch the movie together with a bridger. After the movie is over, immediately or days later, ask the bridger to name seven or eight points in the movie he or she liked best. The bridger likely will recall several elements of the movie that you missed in the first viewing. Bridgers simply are able to absorb more visual information than previous generations.

Captivated by the Tube. Why are the bridgers more adept than older generations at retaining visual information? The answer is simple: they received more training at a younger age. Look at the weekly television viewing times of bridgers:

Weekly Television Viewing for Bridgers
(Shown in hours: minutes per week)

	Ages 12–17	Under Age 12
Total viewing time	21:50	23:01
Monday-Friday, 7:00 A.M. - 10:00 A.M.	:52	2:07
Monday-Friday, 10:00 A.M. - 4:00 P.M.	1:55	3:11
Monday-Friday, prime time	6:57	5:42
Saturday-Sunday, 7:00 A.M. - 1:00 P.M.	:51	1:24
Sunday, 1:00 P.M. - 7:00 P.M.	1:23	1:13

Source: 1992–1993 Nielsen Report on Television

Surprisingly, bridgers are not the worst television junkies. Adult women spend nearly 40 percent more time at the television than teenage bridgers. And adult men spend almost 30 percent more time watching television than bridgers. The difference is that the bridgers' lives have been dominated by television since birth. They are the first generation to have thirty or more channels through which to surf. They are the first group of Americans to be able to watch twenty-four hours of news, sports, weather, or even cartoons with the push of a button.

To understand the bridgers well, we must understand the media which captivated them. That is why we will explore the topic in greater detail in a later chapter.

Shorter Attention Spans. The downside of visual acumen is a decreasing ability to focus on any one subject for a given length of time. Numerous studies have pointed to this phenomenon among the busters. But the bridgers' attention spans will be even shorter.

The media understand this characteristic of bridgers well. Indeed, we cannot be certain if the media created the situation or simply responded to it. Television shows move quickly from one scene to the next. Commercials interrupt the flow for even more manageable consumption.

Bored Silly. I am writing this chapter at a Christian retreat center where I am speaking. The retreat is lovely, and the "down time" has been good for my wife and me. We were glad to get off the fast track of life for a week.

Originally, we had planned to bring our three bridger sons with us, but their we-have-to-go-to-this-basketball-camp commitment interfered with their plans. So grandma is keeping the boys in Louisville.

When I called my boys from the retreat, one of them asked me what we had been doing. I responded that, outside of my speaking commitments, we had walked trails, read books, and, for me, written part of this book. That response was insufficient for him. "But what are you *doing*?" he asked again. I understood his question now. Reading, walking, and writing were not "doing" activities. My son implied that he was glad he had remained in Louisville.

The visual generation has from their births learned that they can be entertained. If they are not involved in some busy activity, they can turn on the television set and be entertained. Anything outside of busyness and watching television or movies is boring. The visual bridgers have not had many opportunities in their lives to do nothing, to relax, to read, or to reflect. They are either busy with an activity or they are watching television.

Read Less. Reading does not capture the attention of most bridgers. These young people may devote over twenty hours a week to television viewing, but they read on the average fewer than five hours per week.[22] The implications for the church are staggering. How will Christians, a people whose lives are devoted to the written Word, reach a generation whose desire to read is less than any previous generation?

Slower Developmental Skills. While the bridgers as a generation can grasp visual images quickly, their verbal skills are weak.[23] The visual generation has some strengths compared to previous eras, but those strengths have a downside to them. Not the least among these downside issues is that bridgers may mature more slowly in emotional, intellectual, and developmental skills.

Money on Their Minds

Bridgers have economic issues on their minds. Though they may not be well-informed about political candidates, if they know one thing about a candidate it is usually related to the economy. Is he or she a tax-and spend liberal? Is the candidate a government-slashing conservative? How will this person affect my economic well-being if he or she is elected?

In chapter 5 we will examine in detail the economic issues which impact the bridgers. For now, let us see at least four reasons *why* this generation has money on their minds.

Reason #1: Materialistic Boomer Parents. The parents of bridgers are poor examples if materialistic preoccupation is considered a negative character trait. The generation that thought they could save the world in the sixties and early seventies became the generation that tried to own the world in the eighties. And the bridger children took note of their parents' priorities.

A key slogan of the 1980s was "You can have it all." The transformation of the boomers from idealists to materialists seemed complete when former hippie Jerry Rubin cut his hair and became a securities analyst. And though the stock market crash of 1987 may have tempered the boomers' zeal to have it all, they had already taught their bridger children a lesson: money is really what matters.

Reason #2: The Downsizing Environment. A Downsizing" has become a word of dread and fear for the bridgers. Though some question the validity of a downsizing crisis—sensing it to be more of a media creation than a new economic urgency—fear of job losses is very much a concern for many adults.[24]

Many bridgers have parents or they know other adults who have been taken off the payrolls of companies in their communities. And if they do not have a close relationship with the casualties of downsizing, they have heard the media hype the issue. Whether or not their fears are justified, their angst is real. Bridgers are money-minded because they fear the money may soon be gone.

Reason #3: Family Deterioration. Single-parent families may be the configuration for a majority of the bridgers at some point in their youth. One demographer estimates that half of the bridgers will live with a single parent before they reach the age of eighteen.[25]

The impact of single-parent families for bridgers is both emotional and financial. A strong correlation exists between single parenting and economic woes. In 1989, 55 percent of all children under six whose families had income below the poverty line were living with single mothers.[26] As the number of bridgers living in one-parent homes increases, so do the concerns of these young persons about matters of money.

Reason #4: Their Own Materialistic Values. The materialistic values of the bridgers cannot be explained solely by greedy boomer parents. Indeed, the issue is much too complex to offer such a simplistic solution. Many bridgers also have been exposed to the ways of consumerism at an early age through the influences of the media, politicians, and a myriad of other forces.

For example, one study of younger bridgers, ages eight to twelve at the time of the study, found that they had $8 billion of their own money to spend annually. Virtually all of their money is discretionary, so the youngsters spent about $6 billion each year. By the time a bridger reaches age ten, he or she is making more than 250 visits to a store each year to make a purchase.[27] The bridgers have more money than any generation in history, but, paradoxically, they have more money worries.

Skeptical Minds

The bridgers as a generation are not sure what to believe or whom to trust. Some researchers are already calling them the "uncommitted generation" and "the anti-institutional generation." Both labels are unfounded and premature.

If the bridgers appear anti-committal or if they seem to be anti-institutional, it is because they are dealing with mixed signals. They prefer to trust institutions and they are willing to make commitments, but they may not have found anything which they feel is worthy of commitment. Their skepticism is related to an overall public decline in expectations about the future.

A mistake many institutions made with the boomers and busters was to assume that their lack of willingness to commit was an attitude that could not be overcome. The church was foremost among those institutions with such a fatalistic perspective. "We can't expect them [boomers] to commit to anything in our church," one pastor lamented, "so we just take whatever they give us." This attitude is self-defeating and self-fulfilling.

We must not assume that the skeptical attitude of the bridgers is a terminal scenario. To the contrary, an anti-commitment attitude may be a thin veil covering a strong desire to find that person or institution worthy of their commitment. The church lost most boomers for a lot of reasons, but one of the big ones was that the church *assumed* the boomers would not commit to the church's values. We must not make that same mistake with the bridgers.

Politically Confused

We probably never will classify the bridgers with any single political label. They are not (and probably will not be) Democrats or Republicans. They are not liberals, moderates, or conservatives. "There is no political pattern that fits with their system—that's why so few care about or participate in the political process."[28]

The Perot phenomenon, first evident in the 1992 presidential election, may very well become a fixture as the bridgers reach voting age. Fewer and fewer young persons see their identity in a certain political party or ideology. Perhaps more than any other generation, the bridgers will call themselves "independent."

If any descriptive label fits the political reality of the bridgers, it might be "pragmatists." Their outlook focuses on "what works now." Their viewpoint is short-term. One straightforward sixteen-year-old bridger voiced her viewpoint: "If I were voting, I would vote for the candidate who could help me the most today. I'm so pessimistic about the future that I don't even worry about what will happen a few months from now, much less several years down the road."[29]

Thoughts about God?

When we look in greater depth at the faith of the bridgers in chapter 9, we will discover a generation that very much has God on its minds. But perhaps it would be more accurate to say that the generation has some vague spirituality on its minds rather than the God of Scripture.

In a recent conversation with a group of bridgers ages twelve to sixteen, I was surprised to hear their understanding of God. Eric's conversation was somewhat representative of the view of this supposedly Christian group. "You know, to me God means the 'main guy.' And the 'main guy' means different things to different people. I got friends who find God in ways that are totally different from me. But ultimately it's the same—it's God."[30] Even more surprising was the fact that this group was comprised mainly of young people from families with Christian identities.

For the older bridgers, the name of God can cover a variety of experiences and expressions. He may be the one and only God of Scripture, or he may be an undefined universal spirit.[31] If teenage bridgers say that they believe in God, we have no idea what they mean today.

Exclusivism is a great offense spiritually to the majority of the bridgers. Thirteen-year-old Mary said it this way: "I get real angry at these Christians who tell me that Jesus is the only way to heaven. I mean, what kind of arrogance is that? Do they really believe all the rest of the world is going to hell?"[32]

Again, other research confirms this anti-exclusivistic attitude among bridgers. "From a spiritual point of view, the all-roads-lead-to-heaven mindset is deeply ingrained. Half of all teenagers state unapologetically that is doesn't matter what faith you embrace since they all teach similar lessons."[33]

Unlike the majority of previous generations, this seventy-two-million strong population group is not growing up in homes that even claim to be Christian. Parental influence to point these young people to the Savior is negligible at best.

But the bridgers do have some vague notion about God on their minds. The reason "God" is on their minds, however, is that all other avenues to fulfillment seem empty. Money may be on their minds, but it seems to be a matter of economic survival more than a desire for extravagant living. Achievement in the world may be a goal, but the bridgers tell us that, even if that goal is reached, it will bring only economic security, not deep, inner fulfillment. And as a generation, they have yet to see cause for hope in any institutional system, whether it be governmental, religious, educational, or economic.

The bridgers have "God" on their minds. The key question is: What kind of God will they find?

The Church Responds

At the end of each chapter of this book we will see possible ways the church can respond to the bridgers' scenario described within that chapter. Each section is brief, with the intention of the final chapter providing a more detailed examination of ways the church can reach the bridgers as we enter a new century.

The trend in generational issues for the church is to discover where each generation is economically, emotionally, socially, and religiously, and then "fit" the church to meet their needs. You will notice that I resist such accommodation throughout this book. I am not saying, however, that churches should be ignorant of generational issues and insist that the 1950s church paradigm is meant for everyone.

Cultural awareness and sensitivity have long been understood as a requisite to foreign missions. One cannot expect to reach a culture for Christ unless that culture is studied and understood. For many years, America in the majority was largely a monocultural Western Christian society. Such is no longer the case, particularly with the bridgers. Their values are not the values of Scripture. We must understand this generation if we are to reach them.

Understanding, however, is not synonymous with total accommodation. We must not bury our heads in the sand, but we must understand that true seekers are not coming to the church to find a world just like the one in which they live. Indeed, the church would have difficulty replicating the bridgers' world, even if it desired to do so.

While we certainly need the awareness that the bridgers are growing up in a culture different from our own (for example, they are certainly more visually oriented than previous generations), we should not try to be identical to their culture. One Christian researcher said it well: "But let's get some perspective. Attracting kids to church does require relevance in style, but it is not the performance itself that will cause them to embrace Christ and His Church. If kids want a show, better venues and more professional performers are available. If they want hot music, MTV and FM radio serve it up 24 hours a day. Having a separate stylized Sunday morning experience is very thoughtful and probably the most appropriate way of appealing to kids, but no matter how great a church service may be, sleeping in would be preferable. *Kids respond to people who care about them.*"[34]

Our research shows that the baby boomers returned to the church in large numbers in the 1980s, perhaps as many as twenty million. Sadly, that same research shows that the boomers exited the church by the same number or even greater in the 1990s. One boomer's comment is representative of those who returned only to leave again: "I came back to church looking for something to fill a void in my life. And I was impressed by the way the church had changed to have music and worship more relevant to the world I am familiar with." But his comments on why he left are noteworthy: "After two years I gradually attended less and less, until I left the church completely. You know, *I came to the church seeking something different, but I left because it was not much different than the world I knew.*"[35]

We must not make the same mistake with the bridgers. While we must be aware of their culture and make some adjustments accordingly, we must also challenge them with the claims of Scripture and the gospel of Jesus Christ. In light of the issues on the minds of the bridgers, how then can the church respond?

Teach Them/Challenge Them

Later in this book we will discuss the issue of getting bridgers into the church for the first time. For now, let us look at one issue once they have begun to attend our churches.

In a fascinating book about the decline of mainline churches, three authors conclude that the failure to challenge young people biblically was a major factor behind the denominations' woes. "Today Presbyterians should not bemoan the lack of faith and church commitment exhibited by their youth, since they have no one to blame but themselves. No outside power forcibly pulled their children away from the faith. No conquering army or hostile missionaries destroyed the tradition. The Presbyterians made the decisions themselves, on one specific [doctrinal] issue after another, over the decades."[36]

In a recent study, we showed that the great majority of the strong evangelistic churches in our nation used strong Sunday Schools as a method for reaching and discipleship.[37] Bridgers may require some new teaching approaches, particularly teaching that is more visually-oriented. But, above all, bridgers are hungry for challenges. They may want education for economic reasons, but such an explanation would be an oversimplification. They are hungry to learn, to be challenged, to be shown that biblical Christianity is different from anything else they may be seeking.

Now is *not* the time to dumb down our teachings and expectations. More than ever, our Sunday Schools need to increase expectations and challenge the bridgers with the cost of discipleship clearly taught in Scripture. The bridgers have minds that are eager to grasp these truths taught in our Sunday Schools and discipleship groups. Whether the bridgers are still preschool age or preparing for college, our churches must teach them the counsel of God in the Bible. The Holy Spirit will then do His role of teaching and convicting. Psalm 78 speaks clearly to our role.

> *O my people, hear my teaching;*
>   *listen to the words of my mouth.*
> *I will open my mouth in parables,*
>   *I will utter hidden things, things from of old—*
> *what we have heard and known,*
>   *what our fathers have told us.*

> *We will not hide them from their children;*
>   *we will tell the next generation*
> *the praiseworthy deeds of the LORD,*
>   *his power, and the wonders he has done.*
> He decreed statutes for Jacob
>   and established the law in Israel,
> which he commanded our forefathers
>   to teach their children,
> so the next generation would know them,
>   *even the children yet to be born,*
>   *and they in turn would tell their children.*
> *Then they would put their trust in God*
>   *and would not forget his deeds*
>   *but would keep his commands.*
>
> Psalm 78:1–7 (emphasis added)

A Solution for Stressed-out Bridgers

Before I became a Christian, I worried about everything. Stress was common for me as a child for even the smallest of issues. Some time after I accepted Christ, I began to discover the truth of walking in the Spirit and His peace. One of my favorite passages was Philippians 4:4–7: "Rejoice in the Lord always. I will say it again: Rejoice! Let your gentleness be evident to all. The Lord is near. Do not be anxious about anything, but in everything, by prayer and petition, with thanksgiving, present your requests to God. And the peace of God which transcends all understanding, will guard your hearts and your minds in Christ Jesus."

Bridgers will learn, as they listen to uncompromising biblical teaching, that the stressful world in which they live can be overcome by the One who has overcome the world. The simplistic solution that "Christ is the answer" is profoundly true. Only by accepting Him will people discover that peace which transcends all understanding, even in the midst of a stressful world and difficult problems. Rather than soft-pedaling the gospel message, we must present it clearly and without compromise. They must know that peace can never be found outside of Jesus Christ.

An Answer to the Independence/Dependence Struggle

Bridgers have more independence than any previous generation at such a young age. But, as we saw earlier, many would like more clearly defined boundaries. And many would like the opportunity just to be children dependent upon others.

Again we Christians have the answer to their needs, if only we would break the barriers to tell them the good news of Jesus Christ. We have a message that only in total dependence upon Christ can they find true rest and joy. Jesus said, "Come to me, all you who are weary and burdened, and I will give you rest. Take my yoke upon you and learn from me, for I am gentle and humble in heart, and you will find rest for your souls. For my yoke is easy and my burden is light" (Matt. 11:28–30). God's yoke clearly defines our boundaries: we go where Christ goes.

Christ Is the Only Way

The research on bridger religious attitudes indicates that many will resist strongly the notion that Jesus Christ is the only way of salvation.[38] Indeed, the concept of exclusivism may be offensive to many of them. When Jesus said, "I am the way and the truth and the life. No one comes to the Father except through me" (John 14:6), He was not being "seeker-friendly" as we commonly use the term. The Savior, to the contrary, was issuing a clear call that any other person or religious system was false and a sure path to hell!

Bridgers may resist exclusivism. They will not be the first group to do so over the past two thousand years. But if we really love them and have a biblical theology of lostness, they will see our love and concern. And then we depend upon the work of conviction by the Holy Spirit. This is the way we will reach the minds and hearts of the bridgers.

The World They Knew

Highlights

- The bridger generation does not have the "web" of extended family or friends that previous generations knew.
- The bridgers will replace the boomers as the generation upon which the nation gives its attention.
- The bridgers could be called "the media generation."
- The bridgers could be called "the rights generation."
- The bridgers are growing up in a world that has devalued human life.

Their place in the record books is already secure. They may one day surpass their parents to become the largest and most influential generation in history.

Susan Mitchell,
on the seventy-two million bridgers
born between 1977 and 1994

I was in Mrs. Cook's third grade class during math. Mrs. Ogletree, the principal, came to the door of our classroom and whispered something to Mrs. Cook. The look on my teacher's face was something I will never forget. Her face turned pale and her jaw dropped. For a moment I thought she might cry. Then, perhaps realizing that more than twenty young children were watching her, she regained her composure.

Mrs. Cook went to the front of the classroom. She spoke softly but with firmness. "Boys and girls, I want you to pay careful attention to what I am about to say. History has been made today, and it is very important that you listen closely and observe everything that will take place in the next several days." She paused. Then Mrs. Bootie Cook said five words that will be forever etched in my mind: "The president has been shot." The date was November 22, 1963.

The assassination of John F. Kennedy has been described as a pivotal moment in the history of our nation in general, and in its impact upon the baby boomer generation in particular. America lost her innocence that day, some observe. The radical sixties were a natural consequence of the assassination, others postulate. A young charismatic president had been gunned down in a crime that, to this day, still carries many questions and problems. But for my generation, the boomers, that most influential moment is often phrased in a question: "Where were you when JFK was shot?"

Since we are not prophets of the future, we cannot see those moments-to-come which will be pivotal events that will forever shape a generation. For the boomers, assassinations, the Vietnam War, the civil rights movement, and the free-love emphasis have shaped our generation in profound ways. But history has yet to be for most of the bridgers. The majority of this generation has yet to pass through adolescence and into early adulthood.

Though we cannot predict precise events of the future, we can see clear and discernible influences that are shaping and will shape the lives of the bridgers. Two points must be made, however, about these shaping influences which may become "the world they knew."

First, the list is not exhaustive. Indeed, the shaping influences of which you are about to read may not be the most significant. But few would argue that the influences are unimportant.

Second, the influences noted are, for the most part, pessimistic. Indeed, the theme of my entire research appears pessimistic. And being an optimist by nature, I write these observations with a great sense of trepidation.

Yet the bridgers do, and probably will continue to, live in a difficult world. My hope is not based on the circumstances of the world, but upon the One who promises life more abundantly. It is with that hope that we project the major influences on America's second largest generation.

Ten Shaping Influences of the Bridgers

Four of the most dominating influences affecting the bridgers today are crime, the media, economic issues, and the changing shape of the family. Because these issues are so pervasive, we will examine each of them in detail in following chapters. For now, let us take a cursory glance at each of the ten influences that are shaping the bridger generation.

Shaping Influence #1: Disappearance of "The Web"

Richard Louv reflects how children of yesteryear had webs of support upon which they could depend. He recalls his own web of security: "As a boy growing up in a troubled family, I sensed that I could get much of what I needed from the web—neighbors to watch out for me on the street, schools that cared, and an understandable community in which to prove myself."[1]

For the bridgers, all parts of the web are disappearing. Even that first and vital part, the immediate family, is not the web of support it was in earlier years. And while we will examine that issue further in the next chapter, for now we must grasp the hard truth that the strength and center of the web at best has become dysfunctional, and at worst is disappearing.

Even if the immediate family were Ozzie-and-Harriett reality in most homes, the positive influences beyond the home are fast disappearing. James Cromer, director of the Yale Child Study Center, sees this breakdown as a factor nearly as critical as the breakdown of the nuclear family. According to Cromer, the pervasive influence on children is parents until the children are about nine years old. The influences from outside the home then begin to dominate. In the past, children could depend upon extended families, healthy neighborhoods, churches, and community groups. "Between home and school, at least five close friends of my parents reported everything I did that was unacceptable," Cromer said "They're not there anymore for today's kids."[2]

My wife, Jo Rainer, grew up in a rural area with as many as nine grand-parents, great-grandparents, and great-great grandparents living nearby. She recalls when her mother returned to college and was away from home for many hours each day. "I never experienced the latchkey syndrome. When I came home from school I would just go to Nanny's, Granny's, or Mama Dyke's home. They were very much a part of the family I knew."

Now Jo is concerned about the generation of our three boys. That strong web of support that extended to several families just is not available for the bridgers. Many young people find their only webs in gangs or groups of youth looking for trouble.

As we will see in detail in the next chapter, some of the realities of today's American family include:

- The family size is smaller.
- More young children are the innocent victims of divorce.
- Step-parents are now a part of the social mainstream.

- More and more children are born and raised out of wedlock.
- More and more families are headed by single parents.

Rachel speaks for many bridgers: "I was in the third grade when my parents got a divorce. My first reaction was I was sad and I wanted them to stay together. Even though I knew they didn't really get along, I just wanted my family." Rachel then recalls her initial response. "I cried for three straight hours, and after that I just blanked it out and really can't remember the things that my mom or dad told me that I did or what happened to me. I lived in [another city, in the East] until I was six and then we moved here, and there was a custody fight and a divorce. So I just want some stability in my life."

Rachel continues: "A couple of weeks ago I asked a new friend of mine if he lived with his mom or his dad. And he kind of went, 'What?' I was embarrassed. To me, it was just a given that he lived with one of them, and he said, 'I live with both my parents.' And it was like, 'Oh, oh, I forgot.' People can still be married you know. It never even crosses my mind that somebody's parents might still be married."[3]

The Rachels of this generation are fast becoming the majority. What will the disappearing web mean for them?

Shaping Influence #2: The Important Generational Attention

One of the reasons that the baby boomer generation continues to be self-serving is that everyone has told them how important they are. After all, they are seventy-six million strong, the largest generation in America's history. More books have been written on the boomers than any other generation. More attention has been given to this generation by marketing and advertising agencies, by politicians, and even by the church. The generation has been told by many, and they believe it, that the world revolves around them.

The bridgers will receive this same level of attention. It is just a matter of time before the second largest generation in America's history hears how important they are. Demographers already recognize the bridgers' significance. Writing in *American Demographics*, Susan Mitchell notes: "The youngest Americans are opinionated consumers before they even learn to speak. . . . Their teenage brothers and sisters already exert a heavy influence on music, sports, computers, video games, and dozens of other consumer markets. Yet the consumer power of today's children is just the first ripple of a huge wave."[4]

But Mitchell sees the bridgers' influence extending beyond consumer markets: "Americans aged 18 and younger will form a generation as big as the original baby boom. Like the baby boom before them, their huge numbers will profoundly influence the markets, attitudes and society. Their true power will become apparent in the next five years as the oldest members come of age. Their habits will shape America for most of the 21st century."[5]

The boomers responded to such attention with narcissistic vengeance. Let us hope and pray that their children will see the mistakes of their parents, and turn their influence in more altruistic directions.

Shaping Influence #3: Economic Uncertainty

The boomers were told that they could have it all, to go for all the gusto they could get. The busters were told that it was all gone. The bridgers are being told both stories.

A clearly different economic environment existed for the boomer and buster generations. The boomers, as a rule, enjoyed affluence, prosperity, and economic hope. The busters, however, entered adulthood without the economic euphoria of the previous generation. Theirs was the generation that first heard about the inevitability of layoffs, downsizing, and declining income. Their generation recalls the story, whether real or apocryphal, of the Ph.D. pumping gas.

Enter the bridgers. The bridgers come into an economy that seems basically healthy, but where major shifts are taking place. Now government itself is downsizing. State budgets are being balanced, and the balancing of the federal budget is no longer the rhetoric of the alarmists or extremists. It is an idea that has unstoppable momentum.

The bridgers will thus be taught that the economic health of our nation is sound, but only so if everyone makes necessary sacrifices. The federal government is no longer the employer of choice nor the provider of cradle-to-grave benefits. Each person is on his own. This generation may not fear the economic crashes that the busters anticipated, but they will not have the economic certainty and comfort of the majority of the boomer generation.

Though the bridgers may be less idealistic than the boomers, they seem to have a healthy realistic approach to the economy. As we have seen, one-half of the boomers in 1971 indicated that they planned to go to college to earn more money. By 1993, however, three-fourths of the older bridgers were making their college plans based on the desire to increase their earning power.[6]

Not only are the bridgers receiving mixed signals about their economic future; different segments of the generation are receiving vastly different messages. This next baby boom is the recipient of a growing poverty rate. The growth in the poverty rate has been steady, from 16 percent in 1977 to 23 percent in 1993.[7] The bridgers are truly a generation of haves and have-nots.

A disconcerting aspect of the poverty-rate statistics is the disparity among white children and black children. Eighteen percent, the proportion of white bridgers who are poor, seems particularly high. But 46 percent of black children live in poverty, an alarmingly high rate.[8] For black children, the poverty rate has not been below 40 percent since 1959, when the Census Bureau first began such measurements.[9]

The significance of the high poverty rate among black bridgers is exacerbated by the growing proportion of blacks in America. African-Americans comprised 11 percent of the original baby boomers, but they account for 15 percent of the bridger generation (see chart 3).

Thus the economic environment for the bridgers will be mixed. For at least a portion of the generation, their view of the economy will be one of cautious optimism. But a significant number of bridgers will only know poverty throughout their childhood. Their sense of economic security will be severely strained by both their actual poverty and the financial chasm that exists between them and their more affluent bridger peers.

Shaping Influence #4: Emergence of the Media Generation

At least one generational observer thinks that the media-influenced bridger generation will reap some benefits as they saturate their minds with television (particularly MTV), movies, videos, CDs, and radio. He notes, "Many people bemoan the time young people spend in front of a TV set. . . . With all of those TV/MTV/video hours, young Americans take in information visually as never before, and they are adept at visual interrelationships of objects and images."[10]

But even this optimistic assessment is tempered with hard reality: "Conversely, they are less-developed verbally and interpersonally. They drink in visual information quickly, and have a far quicker boredom trigger."[11] So even among the less-pessimistic viewpoints, the experts are concerned about the effect of the media upon the bridgers: "Their attention spans are shorter, and they have been instant-gratification-trained to expect information to be delivered comfortably and appealingly. They read less than they used to also— today's college student averages one book for pleasure every three months."[12]

The boomers had network television as their primary media fascination. But the bridgers have a plethora of visual and audio fetishes, and all we can

Chart 3

Racial Composition of the Boomer Generation

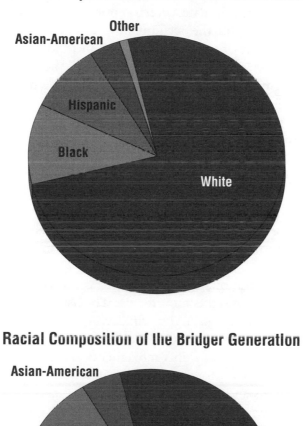

Racial Composition of the Bridger Generation

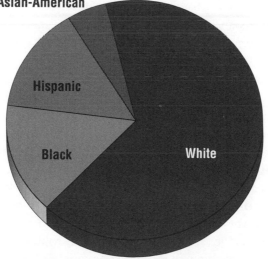

say with certainty...

say with certainty at this point is that the media impact will be strong and pervasive in this huge generation. Unfortunately, most of the evidence today indicates that the negative influences will far outweigh the positives.

Perhaps the latest area of concern is the effect of violent television shows on children's behavior. To date, several reports have demonstrated at least a casual relationship.[13] But the accumulating evidence indicates a clear link between the amount of television watched and increased behavior problems.[14] Watch for increasing parental pressure to control television violence, such as the recent cry for the "V-chip." Most of the pressure, however, is directed at media and government leaders. Few parents of the bridgers seem to realize that they are the ones who should influence and direct their children's behavior.

Shaping Influence #5: Preoccupation with "Rights"

For the boomers, the civil rights movement was a dominant and pervasive influence during their adolescent years. Most of the baby boom adults recall with vivid memories the resounding words of Martin Luther King: "I have a dream. . . ."

The bridger generation, however, sees the rights of African-Americans as just one in a mosaic of rights movements. The list seems to grow each day: civil rights, gay rights, animal rights, children's rights, criminal rights, ethnic rights, labor rights, women's rights, and so on.

Two perspectives on the rights movements are heard by the bridgers in their adolescence. The dominant perspective is that all of these groups deserve their rights and have every "right" to demand them. The emphasis is on "what have you done for me lately?" instead of, "what can I contribute to this world?"

Another perspective, not nearly as influential as the former, insists that rights cannot be granted freely without accompanying responsibilities. Such a viewpoint, contrary to its critics, does *not* imply that a group be treated unfairly or unequally. Rather, it is concerned that the pervasive rights mentality may influence a generation to seek its own pleasures and privileges without responsibilities. Some fear that an entire generation may reach adulthood expecting favors and protection, but having no concept about serving others.

Perhaps this concern is most noticeable among evangelical Christians. Evangelicals take the words of Christ seriously and literally when He said, "And anyone who does not take his cross and follow me is not worthy of me. Whoever finds his life will lose it, and whoever loses his life for my sake will find it" (Matt. 10:38–39). The servant mentality that Jesus advocated is evident throughout Scripture. Another example from the words of Christ notes His emphasis: "Whoever wants to become great among you must be your servant, and whoever wants to be first must be your slave—just as the Son of Man did not come to be served, but to serve, and to give his life as a ransom for many" (Matt. 20:26–28).

If present trends and directions continue, the great majority of the bridger generation will not be asking what they can do for their country; rather, they will be asking what their country has done for them lately. And though a self-serving mentality was evident among some boomers, the bridgers may demonstrate such an attitude to the greatest extent of any American generation.

Shaping Influence #6: Disappearance of Moral Boundaries

Many of the problems in the boomer generation were related to immoral behavior. They had behavioral patterns that were contrary to their parents' teachings. Many of them did wrong, but at least they knew that what they were doing was wrong.

The busters who followed were largely like the boomer predecessors. Most who engaged in wrongful behavior did so with a clear understanding of right and wrong. Some simply made immoral decisions rather than moral decisions.

In an ironic way, we can celebrate the concept of immorality among the boomers and the busters. At least the majority in the generation could define moral or immoral behavior, even if they chose immorality. At least they knew right from wrong. The bridgers know no such boundaries.

For the first time in American history, an entire generation will grow up without certain moral values. Look at some of these attitudes in a survey of older bridgers:[15]

Statement	Agree	Disagree	Uncertain
What is right for one person in a given situation might not be right for another person in a similar situation.	91%	8%	1%
When it comes to matters of morals and ethics, truth means different things to different people; no one can be absolutely positive that they know the truth.	80%	19%	1%
Lying is sometimes necessary.	57%	42%	1%
The main purpose of life is enjoyment and personal fulfillment.	64%	36%	0%

The bridger generation clearly has no certainty of right and wrong. The reasons behind the growth of an amoral generation can best be understood in the development of moral standards of previous generations.

The builders, born before 1946, accepted (and still do today) basic Judeo-Christian principles to discern right from wrong. They believe that the Bible is a moral guide for life today.

The builders' children—boomers and older busters—withdrew in large numbers from church and other Christian activities. Without the influence of the church, they began to engage in activities clearly defined as immoral by their parents. They did have the absolute standards of their parents' morality, but they accepted them in theory rather than in practice.

But the bridger generation had neither a moral standard, such as the Bible, nor a moral example in their parents. Their understanding of right and wrong is fuzzy at best. An entire amoral generation will soon enter adulthood.

Sexual activity is just one example. Recent data from the U.S. Center for Disease Control indicate that 40 percent of ninth graders, 48 percent of tenth graders, 57 percent of eleventh graders, and 72 percent of high school seniors have had sexual intercourse.[16]

These discouraging numbers become even more dismal when one examines the age at which kids become sexually active. High school boys who are sexually active report that they lost their virginity at an average age of 13.2, while sexually active girls indicated an age of 14.6 years.[17] One doctor reported treating girls at age eight and nine years old for severe vaginal injuries resulting from sexual experimentation.[18] And most early attempts at intercourse are typically preceded by other sexual activity such as fondling and oral sex.[19]

But these bridgers as a rule cannot give a clear reason why they should *not* be involved in such behavior. Amorality among these children will soon reap disastrous consequences.

Shaping Influence #7: Rising Violence

This generation has members who are both the instigators and recipients of crime. Never in America's history has such a high proportion of one generation been touched by criminal activity.

The influence of crime and violence cannot be separated from the issue of amorality. To bridgers with no clear moral guidelines, even the wrongness of the most heinous of crimes is not readily apparent to some. Even the secular media are beginning to report the consequences of a generation without boundaries. "The most vexing problem is the small minority of teens who kill or maim with little moral compunction. . . . Police officers are encountering more 'kids with no hope, no fear, no rules and no life expectancy,' says John Firman of the International Association of Chiefs of Police."[20]

Sadly, this crime spree is not likely to end soon. In a cover story about teenage crime, Ted Gest writes in *U.S. News and World Report*: "There is scant hope that the pessimistic trends will stop anytime soon. . . . The tragic fact is that it may take an even greater blood bath to force effective crime solutions to the top of the nation's agenda."[21]

As we will note in an upcoming chapter, the issue of crime and violence is foremost on the minds of bridgers. And sadly, many of this generation cannot say with certainty that their aberrant behavior is wrong.

Shaping Influence #8: Vanishing Gender Roles

The momentum began with the baby boomers, but a clearly-established pattern developed by the time the bridgers were born: "The next baby boom is growing up in an era when the shifting sex roles of the 1970's and 1980's have become the social norms of the 1990's."[22] Marketers already realize that many of the bridgers reject advertising that sells a product to a specific gender. Calvin Klein was one of the first companies to offer a product formerly gender defined. Instead of a cologne for men or a perfume for women, they are offering "cK one," a unisex fragrance.[23] "Tomorrow's young men will be more likely to try hair color and jewelry, while women will be more likely to visit the hardware store."[24]

More and more young women are moving into formerly male-dominated arenas such as college sports. While Title 9 is a federal law prohibiting any type of sex discrimination at colleges, it has had particular impact upon college athletics.

Also, for the first time ever in a generation, young women outnumber men at colleges and universities. And women are entering professions traditionally dominated by men, such as medicine and law.[25]

While a large number of bridger females seek advanced educational opportunities for future career moves, a significant minority of women bridgers have a different motivation. Peter Zollo of Teenage Research Unlimited found that bridger girls with stay-at-home mothers will pursue careers for a different reason. "What's driving young women to want to have their own careers is that divorce rates are so high. They don't want to rely on any man," he noted.[26]

Shaping Influence #9: Rapid Change Driven by High Tech

My first adventure on the Internet occurred in 1996. Prior to that time, I could only imagine what the "information superhighway" looked like. But my three bridger sons, Sam, Art, and Jess, had extensive Internet experience. They are still my guide when I get lost in this world of high technology. And they often inform me of new e-mail messages.

For most of the bridgers, the world of high technology will be the world they knew. Computers will be as common as televisions early in the twenty-first century. An article in *The Futurist* magazine noted that numerous technological trends will impact the bridger generation by the time their youngest members reach adulthood. Among the "92 ways our lives will change" due to technological advances, the article noted:[27]

- Infotech will proliferate in the industrialized companies and spread rapidly in other places.
- Infotech will become increasingly portable and smaller.
- Infotech will be implanted in our bodies. "A chip implanted somewhere in our bodies might serve as a combination credit card, passport, driver's license, personal diary, and you name it."[28]
- The costs of high technology will continue to decline dramatically. "Firms may give away computers to get people to try their other goods."[29]
- Rural and resort areas will boom as high tech allows people to work at home.
- High technology will allow children to start formal education at earlier ages.
- The amount of information resources for students doing papers will increase at a rapid pace.
- Global universities will emerge; as a consequence some bridgers may spend little or no time on a university campus as they get a college education.
- Skills and knowledge will become obsolete faster than ever.
- Cash will become increasingly less popular.
- Anonymity in cyberspace will have surprising consequences, both good and bad.
- We will spend more time in the comfort of our homes because information and entertainment resources will be readily accessible there.

While all ninety-two of these predictions may not become reality in the next few years, we can say with certainty that advancements in technology already have had, and will continue to have, a profound impact upon the bridgers. Our uncertainty lies in the impact of change and the pace of change, which increases with each new day. The bridgers will have little conceptual understanding of stability and tradition. The impact of the unbelievably fast rate of change will not be known for years.

Shaping Influence #10: Devaluation of Life

When the Supreme Court decision of Roe v. Wade was decided in 1973, a few courageous voices declared that the taking of a life in the womb in the early stages of pregnancy was just a beginning. Soon, they cried, later-stage pregnancies, infanticide, and euthanasia would follow. But the majority of those speaking out declared that such possibilities were the hysterical musings of religious extremists.

Four years after Roe v. Wade, the first bridgers were born. And it was this generation that grew up seeing the "hysterical musings" become reality. Abortions in late-term pregnancies became more common. By 1996, the U.S. Congress failed to override a presidential veto of partial-birth abortions. These late-term procedures involve piercing the skull of a near-born child and suctioning the brain out of the body. Thirty years ago such a procedure would have been compared by large numbers of persons to a Hitler-like genocide. Today, this infanticide is covered in the papers for a few days; then the news media return to "more important matters."

Jack Kevorkian, "Dr. Death" to some, will be a name of influence to many bridgers. He will be remembered as a "pioneer" in euthanasia through assisted suicide. The stories of those who have died with his assistance were front-page news at one time. By 1996 they had become small items on a book page.

The basic premise of the assisted-suicide movement is that the solution to suffering is to kill the sufferer. "Rights" of the sufferer become the primary issue. "We have a right to die." "We have a right to die with dignity." "We have a right to avoid pain and suffering."

Largely unknown to the bridger generation is the Christian perspective that suffering can be an instrument for God's glory. "Dear friends, do not be surprised at the painful trial you are suffering, as though something strange were happening to you. But rejoice that you participate in the sufferings of Christ, so that you may be overjoyed when his glory is revealed" (1 Pet. 4:12–13).

The slippery slope of assisted suicide has become clearly obvious to the bridger generation. In the Netherlands, where assisted suicides are legal, the law initially allowed the suicides of those with terminal illnesses. Later, legal assisted suicide included those with chronic illnesses. And lately, legal authorities do not prosecute assisted suicides of those who are severely depressed.

The same pattern has developed with Kevorkian. His first "patients" were terminally ill, but later suicide victims included several who were chronically ill but had no terminal disease. The devaluation of life is complete for the bridger generation. On both ends of the spectrum of life, the taking of a life is decided by a subjective "quality of life" argument, based on the whims and prejudices of a person or persons who become judge, executioner, and god.

The bridger generation has largely responded to abortion, infanticide, and assisted suicide with indifference. They are numb to the taking of lives. They have no moral certainty which tells them that it is wrong, and they are raised in an environment where it is the accepted norm. How will the bridgers lead us into a new millennium with this devalued perspective on life?

The Church Responds

In a previous book,[30] I reported on a massive research project on 576 evangelistic churches in America. The results of this study indicated that biblical basics were the key factors in these churches reaching people of all generations for Christ. While innovative methodologies should be considered prayerfully, this study verified that strong biblical preaching, Bible study for all ages, intentional evangelism, and heightened emphasis on prayer were instrumental in reaching people for Christ.

What this study demonstrated empirically is what we learn biblically in the Book of Acts. The apostles gave their attention to prayer and the ministry of the Word (Acts 6:4). The first-century Christians, like the church headed toward the twenty-first century, found themselves in a culture that was morally antithetical to the morals of Scripture. They also found themselves in a culture that strongly resisted any claims of exclusivity by any religion.

And so the church in America finds herself in a similar position. The temptation of the church will be to compromise to the cultural norms of the day. The temptation may be to become "user-friendly" to the point of biblical compromise. But the church must stand firm, both loving the bridgers and insisting on biblical fidelity.

We will see later in this book futher detail about the response of the church. For now, let us see five major themes for the church that will run throughout this entire book.

The Priority of Scripture

Those churches that reach the bridgers will be biblical churches. Their pulpits will be filled with preachers expositing God's Word in its original context, with application to contemporary society. The Bible will be taught to all age groups, that the truths of God's Word may be known to all generations. Though contemporary methodologies will not be ignored or denounced, the emphasis of these churches will be the Bible, as the Holy Spirit does His work of conviction through Scriptures.

A paradigm book on mainline denominations, written by authors in those churches, notes that mainline churches "have lost members because, over the years, beliefs have been changing."[31] Those outside the church are asking why they should be a part of something that has so little conviction and such an anemic desire to educate or indoctrinate the generations. Speaking of the Presbyterian mainline church predicament, the authors note: "What active Presbyterian baby boomers have abandoned is the level of church participation of their parents, and, in many cases, the conviction of the exclusive truth of Christianity."[32]

Two different studies, one on growing evangelistic churches and one on declining mainline churches, both affirm the absolute necessity of strong biblical teaching and preaching to reach a lost culture. For two thousand years God has honored the faithful teaching of His Word to reach cultures that may oppose biblical truths. The church of the twenty-first century must not compromise on this point, lest we lose an entire generation of bridgers.

Willingness to Be Persecuted

For most of her history, the United States has been friendly to Christians. Persecution of the saints has been something heard about in far-away nations in obscure locations. The mood of this nation is changing, however. The values of Scripture are no longer the values of the majority of the nation. Persecution in myriad forms is possible, if not inevitable. For now the question is: Will the church stand firm?

A Heart for Evangelism

In my earlier-mentioned study, we discovered the not-so-startling fact that effective evangelistic churches are intentionally evangelistic! While such a statement may seem self-evident, the fact is that, in the majority of the churches in America, the people do not think about evangelism on a day-by-day basis. Their churches do not emphasize evangelism, and thus the people do not have a heart and passion for evangelism. Churches that reach the bridgers must have people who believe that those without Christ go to hell when they die; that Christ is the only way of salvation; and that the message of Christ's salvation must be shared with urgency and conviction.

High-expectation Churches

In chapters 10 and 11 we will delve into the issue of high-expectation churches. For now, we will simply make the observation that it is easier to join most churches than it is to join a civic organization. Churches as a rule have "dumbed down" membership in their fellowships. Bridgers are aware of the easy believism and no-sacrifice-demanded discipleship implied in many churches. Ironically, these low-commitment youth respond better to a high-commitment church.

Reach the Bridgers, Now!

Between 75 and 90 percent of all Christians in America became believers before the age of nineteen.[33] And nearly 60 percent of them accepted Christ before age fifteen.[34] Yet most books and material about reaching the earlier generations of the boomers and busters were written *after* they became adults. The time of receptivity to the gospel is typically the greatest during adolescence. We cannot afford to wait until the bridgers become adults. We must reach them now.

Where do we begin? Perhaps a good starting point is simply to learn more about America's second largest generation in history. Such is the theme of the next several chapters. But before you reach the end of this book, you will discover that the agenda is far greater than just learning about a generation. I hope you will read and sense the passion that says we must reach them with their only hope, the gospel of Jesus Christ. And we also must realize that time is slipping away quickly. My prayer is that you will read this book with that same passion and urgency to reach the bridger generation before it is too late.

It's a Family Affair

Highlights

- The bridger generation is redefining the meaning of family.
- The bridgers could be called "the fatherless generation."
- The bridgers could be called "the daycare generation" or "the latchkey generation."
- The bridgers have less time with their parents than any previous generation.

I know my parents love me, but they think that I am so bright and capable that I don't need help or attention anymore. I just want people to realize that I do not have a perfect life and that I am lonely. I want people at school to notice me more and like me. Actually, I'm not at all sure what I want.

Sarah,
a sixteen-year-old from New York

Jennifer and Frank, one would think, would have been in a celebratory mood. The year was 1992, and they had just become parents. I was their pastor, and as I walked into the Birmingham hospital room, my expectation was to walk into a room with two young adults expressing unbridled joy. The mood instead was somber and reflective.

Jennifer did have the new-mother glow and pride as she handed me seven-pound, three-ounce Joshua. Nevertheless, the quietness of the movement surprised me. As I held and looked at Joshua, I waited for one of the parents to speak first.

Frank broke the silence. "Pastor, do you think Joshua has a chance of making it in this world?" I could have expressed dismay and bewilderment at his question, but I knew exactly the nature of his inquiry. Both Jennifer and Frank were the products of broken homes. Frank's parents divorced when he was twelve. Three years later his mother, with whom he lived, remarried. Jennifer's parents divorced when she was five. She lived with her mother, who never remarried.

I knew, therefore, the gist of Frank's question. That was the easy part. The parents, children themselves of broken homes, had just become new parents of a bridger son. They knew the traumas of their own childhoods. And they knew that the statistical probability for an intact, traditional home for Joshua was even less than they themselves had known.

But their question was still unanswered. Does Joshua have a chance in this world? The question in the immediate sense was for me to answer. In the larger context, I realized, the question was for the church. How will the bridgers of America cope with the breakdown of the traditional family? And how will the church respond?

Where Have All the Families Gone?

As one who is in churches in nearly forty states each year, I am optimistic about our opportunity to reach the bridgers. Yet I must confess the family situations in America engender reasons for pessimism. Never has a generation of Americans been raised in such difficult family environments. A 1990 special edition of *Newsweek* spoke volumes about this situation: "The American family does not exist. Rather, we are creating many American families, of diverse styles and shapes. In unprecedented numbers, our families are unalike: we have fathers working while mothers keep house; fathers and mothers both working away from home; single parents; second marriages bringing children together from unrelated backgrounds; childless couples; unmarried couples, with and without children; and gay and lesbian parents. We are living through a period of historic change in American family life."[1]

The church in America will see a generation whose family influences will have been unpredictable. And although the influences may be unpredictable, we can expect bad news for many of the bridgers. One generational researcher put it this way: "The data is not yet in on the residual impact of this fragmentation, but a sociological view suggests a direct link with many of the social strains we see every day. Some of the attitudes, stress, alienation, literalness, weaker communication skills, and shortened attention spans are directly related to strains of adjusting to new kinds of families."[2]

Before we ask how the church might respond to the new family configuration, we will first see the seven most significant family influences on the bridgers. Some of the influences, such as the high divorce rate of boomer parents, seem like old news. But our nation has never known a generation where over one-half of the children will live in a single-parent home for part of their childhood.[3] Some of the bad news is news only in the sense of its acceleration in recent years.

The two last influences that will be mentioned may not have a negative impact on the bridgers. It remains uncertain how these influences will be affected by those negative forces which are destroying families by the millions.

The Seven Greatest Family Influences on the Bridgers

We are moving into uncharted territory with American families. How the bridgers will respond to each of the influences is not known. But what the influences are is clear.

Influence #1: Acceptance of Divorce

Divorce is not new to American families. What is new is the increase and acceptance of divorce. In 1960, only seven out of every thousand children under the age of eighteen lived in a family where a divorce had taken place. But about 50 percent of the marriages begun since 1975 will end in divorce. And three thousand bridgers a day see their parents' marriages end in divorce. Simply stated, the United States has the highest divorce rate of any nation in the developed world.

Already we know some of the trauma inflicted upon the bridger children whose parents have divorced. Judith Wallerstein noted in her study that divorce not only hurts the children deeply but also leaves effects that can be noted for a long time. Some of the problems she cites include:[4]

- Half of the bridgers whose parents divorced are entering adulthood underachieving, worried, angry, and with feelings of inferiority.
- Sixty percent of the bridger children feel rejected by one or both parents.
- Four in ten of these bridgers have no goals or ambitions for life.

- Many of the bridgers, particularly the females, will enter their own marriages with guilt and anxiety. These issues will surface in their marriages and lead to multiple relationships and divorce.
- The bridger children of divorce will be more rebellious and present greater discipline problems.
- Emotions of fear, guilt, and depression will be common among the bridger children of divorce.
- These bridgers will be less likely to trust others.

Not only is divorce accelerating in the families of bridgers, divorce has also become accepted among a majority of the generation. The concept of family has become fluid with few standards. Teenage bridgers are redefining the family. As a consequence, they are accepting as normative those behaviors their predecessors have largely discouraged. Divorce, births to single parents, and extramarital affairs could one day be accepted as traditional marriages and values.

We have some understanding of the impact of divorce on our society to this point. From a human perspective, it is frightening to imagine what will be the shape of an entire generation for whom divorce is normative.

Influence #2: The Fatherless Home

Though my memory may have failed me, I can recall only one of my childhood peers who did not have a father at home during his pre-adult years. From 1955 to 1973, I remember one friend whose father died while my friend was in the sixth grade. Though the town of my childhood was small, statistics reveal that my experience was typical.

In 1970, a full 86 percent of children were raised in a home with both parents present. By 1993, however, nearly a third of the bridgers were living in one-parent homes or with other relatives (chart 4). Most of the one-parent homes were fatherless homes.

Though Dan Quayle was ridiculed for his "Murphy Brown" speech when he was vice president, his words about two-parent families are now repeated by some of his previous skeptics. Walt Mueller supports Quayle's observation: "Children who grow through the difficult, challenging, and formative years of adolescence without their dads have a greater risk of suffering from emotional and behavioral problems such as sexual promiscuity, premarital teen pregnancy, substance abuse, depression, suicide, lower academic performance, dropping out of school, intimacy dysfunction, divorce and poverty."[5]

Chart 4

Types of Households, 1970

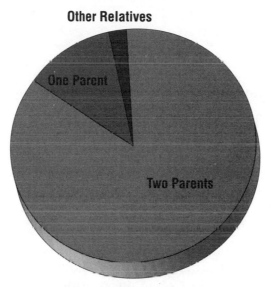

Types of Households, 1993

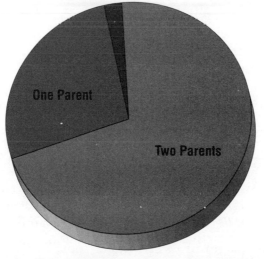

Encouraging signs are evident about fathers committing or rededicating themselves in their parental and spousal roles. Promise Keepers is perhaps the most visible men's movement among evangelical Christians, but others are also growing. By 1997, however, the oldest bridgers were twenty years old, and still that segment of the generation had experienced no significant turnaround in fatherless homes. And a full 70 percent of the bridgers serving time in long-term correctional facilities had no father at home while growing up.[7]

Influence #3: Mothers Working outside the Home

The bridgers are the first generation in America where a majority of the children grew up in families where the mother worked outside the home. So, as we have seen those born between 1977 and 1994 might best be called "the latchkey generation." *Church kids too*

In 1960, some 39 percent of mothers with school-age children were working outside the home. But by 1987, nearly 70 percent of mothers with school-age children were wage earners outside the home. Of those 70 percent, almost two-thirds were in a dual-income situation (husband and wife both working). The other third were single mothers.

The researchers of EPM Communications feel that the effect on the bridgers can already be discerned in many areas, some positive, most negative:[7]

- Because bridgers are less dependent, they can care for others and themselves more readily. But this independence results in their aloofness and distancing themselves from others.
- Because bridgers are required to care for themselves more, they have more information and are more savvy about the world. But they are also less optimistic and less idealistic.
- Because bridgers grew up with their parents gone much of the time, they handle more adult responsibilities at a younger age. But they have "less time for internal growth, for slow maturation, and fewer hours in the dreamy imagination states that many think is a key to a satisfying adulthood."[8]

Influence #4: Decreasing Time between Bridgers and Their Parents

As the boomer parent of three bridger sons, I remember many times when God had to give me a wake-up call about my too-busy schedule. In an earlier book,[9] I related a story about my oldest son Sam confronting me with my negligence of him and my family when he was only five years old. And I have also been influenced greatly by James Dobson and his Focus on the Family ministry.

Yet even with these influences, I often find myself negligent of spending time with my children. Life is hectic. If I have been blessed to have significant persons influence me to give more time to Sam, Art, and Jess, I am likely among the few in my generation with such noble and godly reminders.

Because of dual-income families and because boomer parents have felt that their bridger children must be involved in multiple activities, family time has diminished dramatically. A study in the 1980s noted that working mothers spent an average of eleven minutes each weekday in meaningful activity or conversation with their children. For fathers the number was only eight minutes. The time improved only slightly on weekends: mothers spent thirty minutes a day with their children; fathers spent fourteen minutes a day.[10]

Walt Mueller tells of dividing a high school youth group into small groups to answer this question: If you knew the world was going to end in five minutes and you had the opportunity to say one thing to one person, what would you say and to whom would you say it? Though most of the teenage bridgers took the assignment lightheartedly, Janelle nearly exploded with anger when she responded: "I would walk right up to my father, look him in the eye, and say, 'Dad, you missed it!'"

Janelle was an attractive girl, full of talents and academically gifted. She explained to her youth minister later that evening: "All my father is concerned about is work and reading the paper. He never talks to me or my mom. He never comes to my plays or concerts. He has no interests in my life. He doesn't care!"[11]

Janelle is fortunate in some ways. She is one of the decreasing number of bridgers whose fathers live at home. Researchers are telling us that the Janelles of this world will experience some of the same problems as the bridgers whose fathers are not at home. The problems may not be as severe, but they will be evident nevertheless.

Influence #5: Victims of Family Violence

The church of today and the twenty-first century must be aware that the home itself has become a place of violence and betrayal for many bridgers. Perhaps the most startling statistics are that, by the age of sixteen, one out of every four girls in the United States and one out of every ten boys will have been sexually abused. For most of these bridgers, the abuse will come at the hands of someone closest to them, such as a father. The families of fifteen million bridgers experience violence, much of it the direct result of alcoholism.[12]

I remember well serving as pastor of a church in St. Petersburg, Florida, where a strong and active youth ministry existed. As with almost every youth group, one or two of the young persons were somewhat disruptive. One particular boy, about fourteen years old at the time, demonstrated particularly deviant behavior. Surprisingly to me, the boy acted like he had no desire to be at church, but he was always present voluntarily at every possible church function. Indeed, he typically was the last to leave the church.

Over time I met his parents and learned about the home environment to which he was exposed. Raging fights between the parents were the norm. The police were called regularly by neighbors to break up the violent physical attacks his parents heaped upon one another. And alcoholism was clearly evident with one parent, if not both.

This youth, a buster of the eighties, had a home life like that faced by a significant number of the bridgers of the nineties. Home violence will be common among a large number of the bridger generation. How will the church respond?

Influence #6: Smaller Families/Children Leave Later

American households have been shrinking for nearly two centuries. In 1950, the number of persons in each home averaged 4.76. One out of five homes had seven or more persons. Today only one out of one hundred households has seven or more persons. As recently as 1970, households averaged 3.14 persons. By 1993, the average household size had fallen to 2.63 persons.[13]

Interestingly, the household size may remain steady or increase as bridgers cling to the security of their parents' homes. Like their predecessor generation, the busters, many bridgers are likely to delay leaving the financial security of a home in uncertain economic times. They will therefore keep household sizes higher for a while.

What are the implications of these two major trends related to household configurations? The evidence on household size and its relationship to developmental behavior is hazy at best and conflicting at worst. The experts seem to be telling us that household size alone is less important than how those persons in the household relate to one another.

Nevertheless the church's ministry to families must be ready to deal with the phenomena.

Influence #7: Better Communications? Yes! Not!

Some experts on the bridgers maintain that the good news is that this new generation has perhaps the best lines of communication with parents of any previous generation. Yet another seemingly opposite perspective says that the parents of bridgers and the bridgers themselves are worlds apart. Mueller cites the results of the following survey to demonstrate the enormous size of the generation gap between the bridgers and their parents:[14]

Survey Question	Teens' Response	Parents' Response
Have you had one or more alcoholic drinks?	66% say yes	34% think they have
Have you considered suicide?	43% say yes	15% think they have
Have you ever smoked?	41% say yes	14% think they have
Do you tell your mom about boyfriends and sex?	36% say yes	80% think they do
Have you ever used drugs?	17% say yes	5% think they have
Have you lost your virginity?	70% say yes	14% think they have
Have you thought about running away from home?	35% say yes	19% think they have

On the other hand, demographer Susan Mitchell believes that the generation gap between the bridgers and their parents is relatively small, especially when compared to the boomers and their parents. She believes that the generation gap the boomers experienced was the result of different educational attainment, with the boomers pitted against their less-educated parents.[15]

The bridgers, Mitchell contends, will attain about the same level of education as their boomer parents. "Today, there is little evidence of a comparable gap between the original boomers and their next generation children. While many of the boomers' parents never finished high school, nearly nine out of ten boomers did. This achievement should be realized again with the new generation. One fourth of boomers completed college, and about the same percentage of their children are also expected to obtain college degrees, according to the Census Bureau."[16]

So whose perspective is right? Will the relationship between the bridgers and their parents resemble a family feud? Or will the bridgers relate to their parents in positive and open ways that the boomers never knew? Most likely, truth can be found in both views. The generation gap *does* exist; bridgers are likely to withhold a portion of their lives from their parents. On the other hand, this second largest generational group in history *does* already seem to communicate better with their elders than previous generations. Perhaps the church will seize the opportunities afforded by these more open lines of communications.

The Bridgers Respond

An entire generation, seventy-two million strong, is being shaped by one of the most harmful environments possible. Broken families, divorce, absentee fathers and mothers, diminishing time between parents and children, and family violence are among the negative forces which will play a major role in how this generation will function as adults.

Though it is too early to reach conclusions about the impact of the family on the bridgers (the youngest bridgers were just born in 1994), we can observe the older segment of this generation and make some preliminary comments. And as we paint the picture, we see that it is not pretty.

Sex without Boundaries

The older segment of the bridgers grew up in a sex-saturated society. Outside of divine intervention, we see no reason to believe that the younger bridgers will be in a different environment. This generation comes into a nation where nearly two-thirds believe that sex before marriage is okay if both parties are "emotionally ready."[17]

The bridgers, at least those born before 1983, seem to have a real concern about sexual matters. Three of the teenage bridgers' greatest concerns were related to their sexuality. When asked if the following were concerns or problems for today's teenagers, the numbers were overwhelming:

Percentage of older bridgers who believe the following are concerns or problems for their generation:

	All	Females	Males
One of family getting AIDS	74%	N/A	N/A
Having no sense of right and wrong	N/A	56%	61%
Pressure to have sex	N/A	66%	54%
Being abused by parents	N/A	73%	71%
Fear of pregnancy	N/A	71%	57%

Source: "The Family—Surviving Rough Times in the '90s," American Board of Family Practice

The bridgers present an interesting paradox regarding matters of sexual morality. They have been raised in a largely amoral environment, and they tend to take a liberal view of sexual matters. As long as both parties are consenting and mature, they say, who are we to say it's wrong?

Yet the bridgers also see harmful consequences of no-rules sex. They fear AIDS and pregnancy, and they feel pressured to have sex "before they are ready." But they see little connection between sexual behavior and sexual consequences. They fear AIDS, but they feel personally invulnerable. They fear pregnancy, but that fear seems to do little to inhibit their out-of-marriage sex.

The bridgers are the first full American generation to grow up without social mores and taboos about sex. Even the boomers and busters had some understanding about right and wrong, regardless of what they did about it. But a large portion of the bridger population does not understand morality as previous generations knew it. Perhaps this generation will be responsive to clear teachings about right and wrong. Perhaps the church can be the agent to fill this void.

Living in a Material World

In chapter 5 we will examine the bridgers' obsession with economic concerns. For now, we will say in summary that this generation has learned well the materialistic values of their boomer parents. As the bridgers reach their teens, we see more of them working part-time than any youth generation this century. Many bridgers "have more monthly discretionary income at their disposal than the average adult."[18]

The materialistic values of this generation were learned in the homes of materialistic boomers. The bridgers *are* religious; their religion is wealth and material gain. Even if the nation had unlimited wealth for each family, such a religion would eventually fall. But the bridgers will likely be the first generation since the Great Depression to have a lower standard of living than their parents.

Stress—Depression—Suicide

The bridgers may become the first generation in which the majority of its members take Prozac or other treatments for depression. This generation experiences stress over everything conceivable: schedules, looks, weight, grades, family problems, popularity, and uncertainty about decisions. More youth and children today are victims of depression, eating disorders, and suicide than any previous young generation. The Centers for Disease Control report that suicide rates among American high school students have *quadrupled* in the past four decades.[19] Suicide is now the second leading cause of deaths among adolescents.

Substance Abuse

Some bridgers are coping with stress and depression by experimenting with alcohol and other drugs. Among the older bridgers, those born before 1984, a full 90 percent have tried alcohol for one or all of three reasons: boredom, depression, and stress relief. For many of the experimenters, alcohol consumption has become a lifestyle. And though a slight decline in drug use has been reported in recent studies, still an amazingly high 60 percent of the bridgers will try an illicit drug.

The most frequent reasons for the young people of this generation trying drugs are related in some way to family problems. The drug becomes an escape from the reality of family problems that just will not go away.

No Time for Truth

Perhaps the greatest threat to the bridgers in their family environment is the absence of Christian truth claims. A majority of adults today reject absolute truth. And this lack of belief system is even more prevalent with the parents of bridgers.

The second largest generation in history is growing up in homes with no moral certainty, no absolutes, no sense of *why* right is right and wrong is wrong, and no certain hope for eternal life and God's abiding presence today. Is it any wonder that many bridgers are stressed-out, suicide-prone, alcohol-dependent, and sex-crazed? Without absolutes, they have no way of knowing for certain why anything is right or wrong.

The church is about to be confronted with a generation, that, to a far greater extent than the boomers or busters, is truly without hope. Because this issue is of such importance, we will devote an entire chapter to it later in the book. For now, we can say that never before has the church in America met such an irreligious generation. Christians can despair about the current state of religion or lack of religion in our nation, or the church can see this moment as an opportunity to win a generation before they turn to other belief systems that know not the Savior.

The Church Responds

Before writing this concluding section, I re-read the material about the family environments of the bridgers. I must confess that the research on bridger families left me feeling somewhat gloomy. And I guess I would despair if I did not have the hope of the Lord Jesus Christ. Throughout history, the church has confronted a society whose values are antithetical to the values of Christ. But the church has responded in reaching past generations. How will we respond today? Let us look at three starting points for reaching a generation that has experienced the most tumultuous family environment in our nation's history.

Provide a Safe Haven

Bobby Smith was an alcoholic who had spent several years on the streets of Orlando, Florida. The street talk buzzed about a rescue mission in Leesburg, an hour's drive away. Bobby knew he needed help, so he decided to investigate this place where people like him were welcome.

His expectations were quickly surpassed. For months he worked in the men's shelter, receiving unconditional love and acceptance along with treatment and counseling for his alcoholism. Bobby Smith is now an accomplished artist. His artwork was shown recently in a local arts festival. Said Smith of the ministry he received: "It's given me a new start. What I got here was love and direction, understanding, and patience."[20]

The place of which Smith spoke is First Baptist Church in Leesburg, Florida. Leesburg is a town in central Florida with a population of 25,000. The community has experienced a growth rate of only 6 percent in the past ten years, but First Baptist has experienced an explosion of growth.

The church has more than seventy ministries, one of which Bobby Smith encountered. Pastor Charles L. Roesel has led the church to become involved in "ministry evangelism," a term coined through First Baptist's involvement in multiple Christian ministries. The church has earned a reputation for being a safe haven for those who do not have the security, love, and comfort of strong homes.

People of all walks of life, of various socioeconomic standing, and almost every age have found help and hope in the Leesburg church. First Baptist Church, in many ways, is a model for the churches that will reach the bridgers in the years ahead.

With family problems increasing, many bridgers will be drawn to a place where unconditional love and acceptance abound. They will go to the churches whose ministries say "I care for you" instead of asking for something. A large portion of the bridgers, because of their broken family situations, will be among the walking wounded. The church has a rare opportunity to meet these needs and share the love of a Savior who can meet their greatest need.

Proclaim the Good News

Churches that reach the bridgers will be gospel or good-news churches. Their proclamation will not compromise the message of Jesus Christ. In the turmoil of broken families, bridgers will come to churches that communicate the message that Jesus saves.

Many of the bridgers will bring to church their baggage of guilt and low self-esteem. The growing churches of the twenty-first century will be those that proclaim that sin can be forgiven and low self-esteem can be transformed into high self-esteem through Christ. Bridgers with absentee fathers will hear of an ever-present Father. Those with insecurities will discover the perfect security of the Savior.

Many churches offer well-intentioned, needs-based ministries. Yet, in too many cases, the person in need is never confronted with the truth claims of Christ. While we desire to touch the broken lives of bridgers, our limited human capacities never could provide what this generation ultimately needs. Quite frankly, as every generation before them, the bridgers need Jesus. We have only touched superficial needs when the gospel is not present.

Pastor Roesel explains that ministry can never be separated from evangelism: "Incarnational evangelism, referred to as ministry evangelism at First Baptist Church, Leesburg, Florida, combines word and deed. This kind of evangelism demonstrates Christ's love by unconditionally ministering to persons at the point of their need, hurt, or brokenness. Then the person is confronted with the claims of Christ in an effort to lead the person to accept Him as Savior and follow Him as Lord."[21]

Provide Clear, Biblical Teaching

The seeker-sensitive movement which grew rapidly in the late eighties and early nineties made significant contributions to the American church. It made many Christians aware of the wide cultural chasm that often exists between believers and non-believers. It awakened us to the fact that our language and music of Zion often were not understood by the unchurched. In many ways, therefore, the seeker-sensitive movement has been a missiological movement for which we should give praise to God.

Some churches and Christians, however, took the principle of seeker sensitivity to an extreme. In an effort to make themselves understood and relevant to seekers, they sometimes diluted, avoided, and compromised the clear teachings of Scripture. Indeed, the preaching and teachings were deliberately "dumbed down" in sincere efforts to be understood.

But the pattern of the New Testament calls for an uncompromising teaching of Scripture. The early church in Acts, in the midst of the unbelieving population in Jerusalem, "devoted themselves to the apostles' teaching" (Acts 2:42). And that unwavering stand did not prevent the church from reaching thousands for Christ.

The bridgers *must* hear the clear and convictional teachings of God's Word. They must hear God's plan for the family, for marriages, and for parental responsibility. They must know the consequences of living against God's plan, even if they were raised in an environment that taught otherwise. Our churches must indeed become safe havens for hurting bridgers, but those havens must have clear and convictional boundaries.

The Church—the Family of God

The church that reaches the bridgers will send a clear message that a family is available to love and care for them unconditionally. Though the church must not become a substitute for the immediate family, it must become an alternative for the bridger who has experienced pain and rejection in his or her own family.

But the church cannot simply give lip service to welcoming a generation with many dysfunctional persons. It must provide ministries that touch the heart and the needs of hurting people. In doing so, Christians in their churches may begin to notice change. The new arrivals may come with baggage and problems alien to the older generation in the church. Will the people of today's churches willingly embrace the change needed to break out of their holy huddles? Will they be willing to sacrifice the comfort and security of the way things have always been done for the way God has called them to move? Simply stated, churches that reach the bridgers cannot be content with the status quo.

In chapter 10 we will examine the issue of reaching bridgers now rather than later. In essence, this will require that the church allocate significant resources to student and children's ministries. But reaching these younger age groups rarely has a financial payback. Will churches be willing to expend resources even when those who are reached have little to offer financially in return?

The bridger families *are* largely dysfunctional and deteriorating. But Christians today have something to offer this generation. We are the family of God to which the bridgers may come. Will they find us with loving arms open wide?

CHAPTER 4

A Violent Generation

Highlights

- Bridgers are eight times more likely to be a crime victim than a senior adult is.
- Bridgers could be called "the violent generation."
- The three main causes of bridger crime are anger, parental detachment, and fatherless homes.
- Crime among bridgers is closely related to poverty, education, and race.

The violence-prone youths of the future are now three to five years old.

Barry Krisberg
National Council on Crime and
Delinquency

Police officers in Tallahassee, Florida, had a solid lead on an automobile theft. Working at a nearby restaurant was a sixteen-year-old parolee who had already accumulated thirty-two charges on his juvenile arrest record. After a brief stand-off in an apartment building, the youth was arrested. This time, the prosecutors decided, they would send him for trial in the adult criminal court.[1]

In St. Louis a pregnant fifteen-year-old was shot to death on a school bus. In Miami two boys were charged in the murder of a Dutch tourist who mistakenly found herself in "their" neighborhood. And in New York, a young mother fell to her death when a fifteen-year-old boy tried to steal her $60 earrings.[2]

But the crimes of youth and against youth are not limited to large metropolitan areas. In rural Ohio, a two-and-one-half-year-old girl was killed by two boys, ages six and ten. Nancy Slaven Peters, the mother of the murdered girl, became livid when authorities refused to give her any information about the suspects because of their ages.[3]

Recently a focus group of fourteen youth discussed the issue of crime. Each of these young persons, ages nine to sixteen, was very active in his or her church. When they were asked if they had ever committed a crime, or if they had a close friend who had committed a crime, all fourteen youth affirmed one or both scenarios.[4]

The New Criminals and Victims

We would prefer to disregard the hard facts about crime in the bridger generation. And parents, such as myself, of middle-class, intact-family backgrounds, would like to believe that the world of violence and young criminals is elsewhere—that our own children are removed from such problems. But the reality is that crime is a growing concern for the bridgers. No socioeconomic group nor comfortable suburbanites are exempt.

Contrary to conventional wisdom, young persons are more likely than senior adults to be the victims of crime. For example, the victimization rate among sixteen- to nineteen-year-olds is 173. (That means that for every 1,000 people in this age group, 173 people are crime victims each year.) For senior adults age sixty-five or older, the victimization rate is just 21.[5] Older bridgers are *eight times more likely to be a crime victim* than a senior adult is. The bridgers' higher victimization rate results from several factors. According to surveys, older Americans have a greater fear of crime and are, therefore, more likely to be cautious. Young persons have always tended to have a sense of invulnerability and are therefore much less cautious.[6] The bridgers are no exception, although they seem to have a greater awareness of the reality of victimization than previous young generations.

Three out of four bridgers say that one of their major fears is "someone in the family being a crime victim."[7] Several later studies indicate that the bridgers are indeed worried about crime. The Centers for Disease Control find that twenty percent of high school students carry a gun, knife, or other weapon, with the intention of using it if necessary.[8] And the American Board of Family Practice found interesting behavioral patterns among older bridgers:[9]

- 84 percent call home to say they have arrived at their destination.
- 83 percent take a friend when they have to travel through an unsafe area.

- 77 percent avoid parts of town they feel are unsafe.
- 58 percent avoid wearing clothes that appear expensive.
- 20 percent take self-defense lessons.
- 14 percent carry a chemical spray such as mace for self-defense.

Who are the criminals that are engendering so much fear among the bridgers? Who are the murderers, thieves, and rapists that are increasingly terrorizing the second largest generation in America's history? Increasingly, the bridgers are becoming victims of other bridgers. On a scale that few adults comprehend today, the bridgers are at war with one another.

The Teenage Time Bomb

The March 25, 1996, issue of *U. S. News and World Report* contained a lengthy cover story about violent juvenile crime. The cover contained these words: "Teenage Time Bombs: Violent juvenile crime is soaring . . . and it's going to get worse."[10] America is indeed waking up to the reality that her second largest generation will be the most violent ever.

In 1989 alone, the juvenile crime rate increased an astronomical sixteen percent. Very few leaders in our nation realized at the time that the leading edge of the bridgers had turned twelve years old. By 1994, juvenile offenses were *sixty percent higher* than the rate just seven years earlier. This increase in juvenile crime is taking place in a period when the adult crime rate has remained fairly steady (see Chart 5).

Illegal drug use had declined steadily among high school seniors from 1980 to 1992. But by the time the oldest bridgers had reached their senior year of high school, illicit drug use was increasing drastically (see Chart 6). Of course, the correlation between drug use and crime rates is high.

No single answer can explain the rise in drug and alcohol use among the bridgers. Walt Mueller notes nine reasons kids today are getting involved with drugs and alcohol.[11] Five of the reasons have been common for years:

1. Curiosity and experimentation
2. Peer pressure
3. The perception of fun
4. The desire to look grown-up
5. Advertising

But the bridgers are looking at some factors previous generations have not experienced with such intensity.

Chart 5
Youth Violence Versus Adult Violence

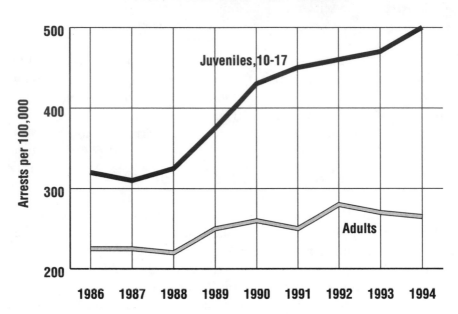

Chart 6
Illegal Drug Use (other than marijuana)
among high school seniors

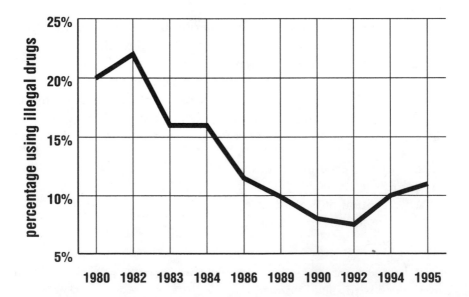

Drugs and alcohol are easier to get today. Data from the National Crime Victimization Survey indicate that two out of three students aged twelve to nineteen reported availability of drugs at their school. The availability varied little in the cities, suburbs, or rural areas.[12] But today one of the easiest sources of alcohol is the parents of the bridgers. Over one-third of seventh to twelfth graders indicate that their parents tolerate or supply alcohol. One youth lamented, "When Mom and Dad put their stamp of approval on drinking, how can a teen believe any other voices that might say teen drinking is dangerous and wrong?"[13]

Increasingly, family problems and the desire to escape are two common reasons bridgers are turning to alcohol and drugs. "Kids who came from homes where there is divorce, separation, an absent parent, discord, marital conflict, poor communication, and abuse are more likely to abuse drugs and alcohol," said one youth expert.[14] But Mueller noted that some families have opposite characteristics: "Conversely, kids who come from homes characterized by love, nurturing, affection, involvement, and marital harmony are less likely to abuse drugs and alcohol."[15]

Another tragic reason that bridgers are turning to drugs and alcohol is the increasing frequency of addiction. The number of adolescents in America who have serious problems with addiction is over three million and growing.[16]

Juvenile arrest rates for weapons law violations more than doubled between 1985 and 1994 (see chart 7). The juveniles represented in the 1994 data are all bridgers, whereas previous years had included some busters.

An anticipated corollary of increased weapons law violations among bridgers is an increase in homicide by juveniles using guns. Murders committed by juveniles *quadrupled* between 1984 and 1994 (see chart 8). In 1994, 82 percent of murders committed by bridgers involved the use of guns.[17]

Among all the alarming trends in crime among the bridgers, perhaps the most disturbing is the rapid increase in murders. The number of juvenile homicide *offenders* in 1994 was nearly triple the number in 1984. The most vexing problem is the increasing number of bridgers who kill or maim with little moral compunction. Judge David Grossman of Cincinnati, president of a national juvenile judges' group, sees a wave of "undisciplined, untutored, unnurtured young people." He notes that "gangs have become the alternative to a nurturing family," and many young murderers "are incapable of empathy."[18]

In fact, the number of the bridgers who are murderers, thieves, or violent criminals is increasing rapidly. The issue has now become one of perception as well as reality. One church-going bridger noted: "I have never

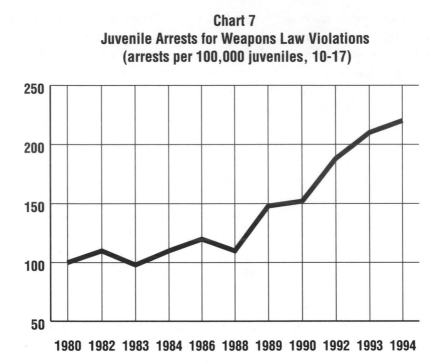

Chart 7
Juvenile Arrests for Weapons Law Violations
(arrests per 100,000 juveniles, 10-17)

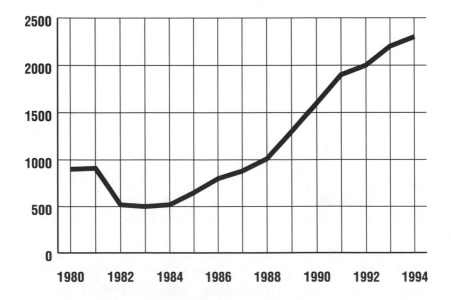

Chart 8
Homicides Committed by Juveniles

seen a violent crime take place, but I hear my friends talk about it from time to time. I feel like I'm in a violent world even though I don't see it."[19]

This bridger's perception is correct. Violent crime among the bridger generation may very well leave its mark through their entire lives. Chart 9 shows clearly the alarming increase in arrests among her peers. Murder, weapons law violations, and aggravated assault have nearly doubled in ten years. Murder has more than doubled in that same time span. And robbery has increased over 50 percent in ten years. We know the statistical reality. The bridgers are growing up in a violent generation. The obvious question is: Why?

Chart 9
Increase in Juvenile Arrests, 1985-1994

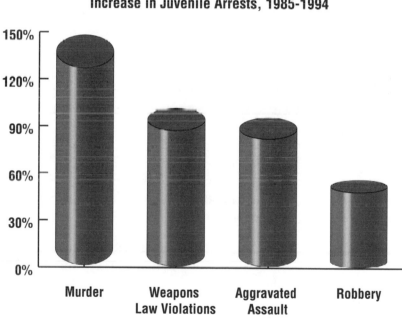

The Reasons Behind the Crimes

The bridgers' increasing involvement in violent crimes belies any simple explanation. Many possible reasons exists, none of which alone would explain the phenomenon. Why would a clean-cut Victor Brancaccio, age 16, kill a woman who criticized his rap music? Why would another teen offer this explanation for paralyzing a jogger who refused to hand over a gold neck chain: "He could have given me his rope [chain]. I asked him twice"?[20]

Moral Uncertainty

The majority of the bridgers today simply do not know right from wrong. Such a statement is not mere speculation, but the confessions of the bridgers themselves. Sixty-one percent of male bridgers and 56 percent of female bridgers admit inability to know right from wrong.[21]

The root of the bridgers' lack of discernment between right and wrong is a lack of belief in absolutes. Bridgers are very situational in their ethical decisions. What may seem right in one situation may be wrong in another. They have no final authority to which to turn. Without a sense of absolutes, we have a generation headed toward moral chaos. It is little wonder that juvenile crime is soaring. Crime is defined as a wrong committed against individuals or society. But many of the bridgers could not give a clear statement of what is "wrong."

Even more disturbing, a majority of self-described born-again Christian bridgers do not adhere to a system of absolute truths. The Christians, one would think, would confidently turn to the Bible as an absolute standard, by which any moral uncertainty could be eliminated. But nearly six out of ten Christian bridgers and eight out of ten non-Christian bridgers deny absolute truth.

The following chart depicts clearly the lack of moral certitude among the bridgers. Perhaps more than any single issue, this uncertainty explains the deviant behavior of many of the bridgers.

Chart 10
Moral Uncertainty Abounds among Bridgers

	Percentage Who Agree	
	Born Again	Not Born Again
What is right for one person in a given situation might not be right for another person in a similar situation.	92%	90%
When it comes to matters of morals and ethics, truth means different things to different people; no one can be absolutely positive that they know the truth.	66%.	87%
There is no such thing as absolute truth; two people could define truth in conflicting ways and both could still be correct.	59%	78%
You know that something is morally or ethically right if it works.	33%	47%

Source: George Barna, *Generation Next* (Ventura, Calif.: Regal, 1995), 101.

Anger

Crime is often the behavioral response to accumulated anger. As bridgers enter adolescence, they experience physical changes that naturally produce emotional fragility. But, more than previous generations, many of the bridgers are living in "chaotic, dysfunctional, fatherless, Godless and jobless settings where . . . self-respecting young men literally aspire to get away with murder."[22] And about one out of five bridgers is "suffering from some type of mental or emotional disorder, such as depression, hyperactivity, chronic drug use, anorexia, and so on, according to the National Academy of Sciences' Institute of Medicine."[23]

Indeed, the crime time bomb may be the result of emotional time bombs. As one surveys the research and insights of today's young people, a plethora of possibilities exists to explain the bridgers' anger:

- Frustration at parents who fail to communicate and give them time
- Absentee fathers
- Increasing poverty rates among children and teens/economic uncertainty
- Frustration at lack of guidelines, certainty, and boundaries
- Family problems

Increased crime is thus partly explained by the emotional time bombs descriptive of many of the bridgers. We must, however, dig deeper into some of these causes of anger to understand more fully the reasons behind deviant behavior.

Parental Detachment

Nearly half of the bridgers say that communication with one or more parents is a very serious problem for their generation.[24] Many bridgers already have spent several years in day care. Those with the most negative views of their experience "felt warehoused, pushed away from their parents."[25] Parental *detachment* indeed seems to be somewhat correlated to the bridgers who get involved with criminal activities. And from the positive perspective, parental *involvement* with children seems to be a key deterrent to juvenile crime.

Walt Mueller notes that "the degree of influence that the world has on our children depends greatly on how involved we become in their lives."[26] Indeed, parental involvement is needed more today than ever before because the culture in which the bridgers live is often in opposition to the values of parents: "Today's parents are faced with raising children in opposition to the dominant cultural message. In the struggle for the hearts and minds of our kids, parents should make an effort to spend even more time raising their children and teens."[27]

Police accustomed to arresting sixteen- and seventeen-year-olds are now picking up twelve- and thirteen-year-olds. A common denominator among these criminal bridgers is parental detachment. University of Pittsburgh police officer John Shamlin notes some consequences in the lives of bridgers: "They have a blatant disregard for authority. They will carry firearms and knives, and they will try to intimidate you."[28] On the other hand, parental involvement engenders greater respect for authority among the bridgers and, thus, less likelihood of criminal involvement.

Fatherless Homes

The father's role is critical in the bridger's character development. Most criminal offenders are coming from homes with absentee fathers. In 1970, 86 percent of children under age 18 lived with two parents at home. By 1993, the percentage of homes with both parents present had dropped to 71 percent.[29]

Bridgers today are far more likely to live with a never-married mother than were previous generations. Children of one-parent homes in 1970 included only 7 percent whose mothers had never married. By 1990, 31 percent of single mothers were never married.[30] Thus, bridgers are increasingly living in fatherless homes, and a growing number have *never* had a father present.

Bridgers and Guns

Crime fighters have noticed an alarming increase in the number of crimes committed by bridgers with handguns. Up to two-thirds of homicides by bridgers involve guns.

States and municipalities are addressing this new phenomenon in various ways. In Boston, police are concentrating their efforts on gun-toting gangs in high-crime neighborhoods.[31] Ten cities have adopted anti-gun programs aimed specifically at the bridger population.[32]

Poverty, Race, and Education

In 1959, the peak of the first baby boom, over one-fourth of the children under age eighteen lived in poverty.[33] By 1993, the poverty rate for children had improved somewhat; 23 percent of children under age eighteen were poor.[34] Though these statistics appear encouraging, the situation for the bridgers is actually getting worse.

The economic position of families improved from 1950 to 1969. Over these two decades the poverty rate for children dropped from 27 percent to 14 percent.[35] By the time the bridgers began the second baby boom in 1977, the poverty rate had risen slightly to 16 percent.[36] In 1993, however, the entire bridger population experienced a poverty rate of 23 percent.[37] As we have previously noted, even more dramatic is the racial difference in poverty rates. Among white bridgers, 18 percent are poor.[38] But nearly 46 percent of black bridgers live in poverty.[39] And, unlike the first baby boom, the bridger boom includes an increased percentage of blacks and a declining percentage of whites. (See chart 11.)

Crime among bridgers is closely related to income levels. The increasing level of poverty rates in this generation would suggest that crime will rise proportionately.

The ticket out of poverty is education, and technological training will become even more important as computers become commonplace in even the lowest-paying jobs. But the poorest members of the bridgers are the least likely to have access to computers in their homes and schools. "Two-thirds of households with personal computers in the home are headed by college graduates earning over $50,000," according to demographer Susan Mitchell. "But computers are present in only 15 percent of homes where the householder did not graduate from college and has earnings of less than $30,000." She further notes a widening chasm in the bridger generation: "Unfortunately the next boomers are divided into haves and have-nots according to their access to technology and the ability to build important skills early in life."[40]

Though crime among the bridgers is not limited to the "have-nots," poverty and lack of education are significant correlative factors to criminal activity. Unfortunately, because black bridgers are more likely to be in poverty, they are also more likely to be a part of juvenile crime.

Society's Response to Bridger Crime

Our society typically has two avenues to address bridger crime. One response is to change the laws that are perceived to be too lenient to the bridgers. Another course of action takes place through the judicial system, with courts and judges responding with tougher sentences and rehabilitative measures. Some states and municipalities are using a mix of law changes, juvenile and adult corrections programs, and volunteer systems.

Chart 11

Racial Composition of the Boomer Generation

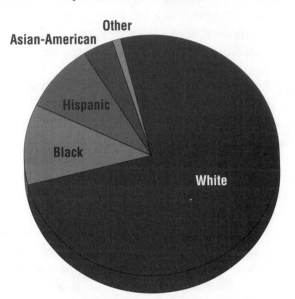

Racial Composition of the Bridger Generation

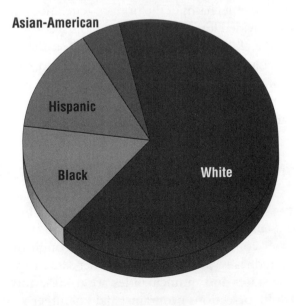

Changes in the Laws

In May of 1993, an infant was hit in the face by a stray bullet while he was watching the polar bear exhibit at the Denver Zoo. Just a few weeks later, six-year-old Broderick Bell was wounded in the crossfire of several bridgers shooting at each other. A store owner was killed a few days later, and his wife was beaten and kidnapped. Then a young elementary schoolteacher, new to the Denver area, was murdered in a robbery attempt.[41]

All of these crimes were believed to be linked to older bridgers. Denver residents still refer to that shocking period as the city's "summer of violence."[42] They began asking "Are we losing control as a city?"[43] Colorado Governor Roy Romer called a special legislative session to address the problem. Within a five-day session several laws were enacted. Juveniles as young as age fourteen could now be charged as adults. Handguns were banned for all non-adults, and a juvenile "boot camp" was established.[44]

Did Colorado overreact to an anomaly? Or is the situation as bleak as the summer of 1993 might indicate? We have already seen the alarming statistics in the rise of crime among bridgers. The number of cases in courts and the number of bridgers in corrections facilities would indicate that Denver neither overreacted nor misperceived the situation:

- The number of cases sent from juvenile to adult courts for trial increased 41 percent between 1989 and 1993, as more bridgers became involved in crime.
- The average stay in youth corrections facilities is now one year for crimes committed against persons, 248 days for drug offense, and 187 days for weapons crimes.
- More than 60,000 bridgers are in custody, many in overcrowded facilities. Almost all of those in custody are males.[45]

Changes in the Courts

In Pittsburgh, the Allegheny County juvenile court has stopped treating crime among the bridgers as an illness. The court system is now more concerned about getting young felons off the streets and holding them accountable for their actions. Young people no longer walk away from serious crimes just because of their age.[46]

The results are encouraging thus far. In 1995 the number of juvenile arrests declined by nearly 30 percent.[47] Public defender Nikki Tufano believes that the permissive attitude of the legal system, particularly the courts, led to increased delinquency among the bridgers. Juveniles rightly thought that they could commit a crime and walk away. But in Allegheny County, says Tufano, the courts have changed. "Kids don't get away with a whole lot here," she notes.[48]

But changes in the laws and courts treat the symptoms without addressing the root of the problem. Even the successful model of Pittsburgh has its challenges. The court has "only two full-time judges, a part-time judge and one court-appointed master to handle a yearly docket of approximately 6,000 delinquent and 1,400 dependent referrals."[49]

We are witnessing a young generation become a generation of criminals and crime. Those bridgers who are not the criminals are often the victims of the crime. We are raising, educating, and providing for the most crime-ridden generation in history. And while tough laws, strict courts, and well-trained counselors are good, they are not the whole solution. The church has a unique opportunity to respond to a most difficult situation.

The Church Responds

Any single explanation for the high crime rate among the bridgers would be an oversimplification. Those reasons delineated at the beginning of this chapter, however, do provide a base from which the church can respond to this violent generation.

"Old-Fashioned" Time

When we see anger, moral uncertainty, and disregard for authority common among bridgers, we also are seeing young persons hungry for time and real relationships with adults. Those youth often have little or no such relationship with their own parents. And the void of parental concern is not limited to lower-class gang members. Listen to the story of Sarah, a sixteen-year-old from an upper-middle-class home in New York:

> My mother always compares her life to mine, so much that sometimes I feel smothered by her. I cannot talk to my father at all about important things. I never could. My father is home every evening at 6:00 P.M., but my mother is never home. She recently opened a business so she has to work from 9:00 A.M. until midnight. Sometimes she comes home to see me in the afternoons, and sometimes she is around on weekends. Incidentally, my parents do not get along very well.

My mom says that if I get therapy, it will go on my record and may keep me out of Princeton or Amherst, the colleges to which I am applying.

I know my parents love me, but they think that I am so bright and capable that I don't need help anymore. I just want people to realize that I do not have a perfect life and that I am lonely. I want people at school to notice me more and like me. Actually, I'm not at all sure what I want.[50]

Young criminals rarely come from homes where parents spend abundant time with their children. And while the church cannot be a parental replacement, it can be a place where adults give significant time to young people.

Most churches have not chosen to give the time necessary to meet the needs of bridgers. They typically have a few adult youth leaders who meet and do activities with young people in the church. But bridgers need significant one-on-one time. This generation has missed out on appreciable contact time with adults. Churches that reach this generation will need to have a large number of adults dedicated to spending significant amounts of time with the bridgers. To make a difference in reaching bridgers will require addressing this issue immediately.

A potentially explosive issue in bridger-friendly churches will be the arrival of young men and women, boys and girls, who neither look nor behave like the church crowd. Undoubtedly, some churches will decide that significant investments of time in "that kind of people" are neither wise nor financially prudent. But other churches will simply take the path of Jesus and welcome the "unchurchy" bridgers with love and acceptance. They will open their doors wide, without compromising their message or their convictions. And many adults will give significant amounts of time to these starved-for-love-and-attention young people.

While any adult attention is important to the bridgers, wise church leaders also will realize that attention from men in the church may have the most significant impact. "Big brother" relationships, often modeled with success in the secular world, could very well be a dynamic ministry for churches that reach the bridgers. The impact of one godly man upon a bridger will have both lifelong and eternal consequences.

Alternatives for Social Interaction

Many bridgers today find trouble in their freedom and boredom. More than any previous generation, these young people are roaming streets and malls. Some churches already are providing the youth a safe haven that is both convictional and fun. One pastor recently shared with me the story of Brian, a rebellious bridger who came from an unchurched home. Brian was befriended by Josh, a committed Christian youth at the church. Eventually, Brian started coming with Josh to church activities. Soon he was present not only in Sunday services but also in activities throughout the week. Today Brian is a Christian who is influencing many of his former peers.

The pastor of Brian's and Josh's church said that the church became highly intentional about reaching unchurched bridgers. They provided activities and outlets that were both fun and biblically challenging. For example, Brian made his commitment to Christ while on a summer mission trip to help a church in an inner-city.

Bridgers typically respond to challenges. Churches that can be culturally relevant and biblically demanding will be the churches that reach this generation. Bridgers, perhaps even more than the rest of us, like to know that the activities in which they are involved will make a difference in this world and in eternity.

Biblical Teachings

In *Effectively Evangelistic Churches*, I noted that truly evangelistic churches are growing significantly by conversion growth more than by transfer growth.[51] Of the hundreds of possible responses, these churches ranked their intentional evangelistic efforts toward youth as a primary reason for their success.

Of the 576 churches studied, the significant majority indicated that the bridger youth were getting deep biblical teachings. Although the teachings were communicated in a manner that the bridgers understood and could enjoy, the truth of the whole counsel of Scripture was never diluted.

The lessons from these evangelistic churches are extremely important. Many bridgers are involved in violence because they have never heard clear black-and-white principles of right and wrong. For many of them, every decision is situational.

But, contrary to the approach of some church leaders who favor a more seeker-friendly approach to bridgers, strong biblical teachings are changing lives in this violent generation.

One youth leader in the evangelistic study stated it well: "We have seen three teenagers' lives changed dramatically from the world of gangs to become regular churchgoers. While we do things at our church to reach out and communicate with these young people, we are always teaching them sound biblical principles of right and wrong."

He concluded with these words: "Seeker-friendly activities are only successful to a point. Eventually and soon the youth need to be exposed to Scripture. There is really power in the Word of God to change lives. We are realizing this truth more every day."[52] May the number of churches that grasp this reality grow in number and strength!

CHAPTER 5

It's the Economy, Stupid!

Highlights

- The work ethic may be returning with the bridger generation.
- The bridgers are uncertain about their economic future.
- This generation is convinced that "things buy happiness."
- The bridgers could be called "the materialistic generation."

> *Today's kids equate happiness with the acquisition of more and more consumer goods, especially luxury items. They express a desire for at least two cars, clothes in the latest style, vacation houses, and recreational vehicles. For many, this track appears to be the only path to happiness and meaning in life.*
>
> Walt Mueller,
> *Understanding Today's Youth Culture*

Nathan is a sixteen-year-old bridger who recently moved from a suburb of Atlanta to a smaller Georgia community. He has joined our focus group to talk about economic issues in general, and personal financial issues in particular. This discussion seems to be the liveliest yet.

The first level of our discussion focuses upon general economic conditions. I am amazed to discover how informed this group of thirteen teenagers seems to be. Their predecessor generation, the busters, were terribly pessimistic about their economic futures. And though this bridger group could not be called optimistic, they are certainly not gloom-and-doom prognosticators.

Perhaps the primary reason for their cautious optimism is that money and becoming financially successful are somewhat of an obsession with the generation. Whereas 40 percent of boomers in 1971 considered financial well-being to be essential, 75 percent of the bridgers have such an aspiration.[1] Half of the boomers in 1971 desired a college education to make more money. But more than three-fourths of the bridgers plan to go to college for that reason.[2]

Nathan seems to fit this mold well. He is neither overly optimistic nor greatly pessimistic about the economic future. But he does seem obsessed with money and material success. "My parents have been talking about money and what they do and don't have ever since I can remember. They have drilled it into my head that making it financially is really important in this uncertain world," he said.

"You know," he observed, "I really do want a lot of things in this world. I want to be able to own my home, to drive a nice car, to have nice clothes. There's nothing wrong with that, is there?

"But I guess in this world of downsizing and layoffs, you really need to cover your rear. If the economy means that there will be 'haves' and 'have-nots,' I want to be in the 'have' group."[3]

Nathan has articulated the feelings of this group. Their nods of affirmation soon become outspoken voices. "I am surprised," I write in my notes. "These are kids raised in Christian homes; they attend church regularly. Where are they getting these materialistic values?"

Several months after the last session with this focus group, I continue to be amazed at the bridger generation's preoccupation with money. No generation in American history has been so concerned about the nation's economy and its impact upon their lives. The caustic but common political slogan, "It's the economy, stupid!" has become the motto of the bridgers. And if we as a nation were surprised that adults today vote more with their pocketbooks and wallets than any other factors, just wait until the bridgers start voting! If current realities continue into the future, we will have a tremendous number of voters whose primary concern is a selfish desire to be better off financially, even at the expense of others' well-being.

Two Groups—Two Economies

Before we delve further into the economic attitudes of the bridgers, we must see clearly that this generation is rapidly becoming two distinct economic groups—the haves and the have-nots. The poverty rate for small children (under age six) is increasing faster than any other group of Americans.[4] This group represents the younger segment of the bridger generation.

Another demographic segment with high representation in the poverty group includes children living with single mothers. More than half of the preschool bridgers living in poverty live with their mothers only.[5] A bridger is five times more likely to live in poverty if he or she lives with a single mother rather than with married parents.[6] "Almost half (45 percent) of new families started in 1990 are at risk for one or more of the following reasons: the mother is under age twenty, the parents are not married, and the mother has not completed high school."[7]

In the "have-not" group, the rate of juvenile violent crime is considerably higher, a topic we examined in some detail in chapter 4. But racial demographics paint the harshest picture. Minority children are much more likely to be in poverty than white children. A black teenager is twice as likely to live in poverty as a white teenager.[8] Thus, black children are statistically more likely than other children to be perpetrators or the victims of violent crime.

This brief survey of demographic data is intended to provide insight into a generation that cannot be stereotyped as one group. As with any generalized study, however, there will be a tendency in this book to give stereotype characteristics of the generation that will not hold up for some individual cases. For the bridgers in particular, many of the demographic and sociological characteristics will not apply to the economic "have-nots." Many of the statements and assumptions made in this book will typically apply to the larger group, the "haves" among the bridgers.

The Work Ethic Returns?

Perhaps unfairly, the buster generation was at times called "slackers," people who neither cared nor tried. Also perhaps unfairly, the boomers often were called the "me generation" because they were perceived to be self-centered and caring little for others. How will the bridgers be characterized?

America's second-largest generation may soon be described as the generation that brought back the work ethic. But the motivation to work hard seems to be more out of concern for economic security than any desire to give their best without regard to rewards.

Walt Mueller tells of taking five girls, all high school sophomores, on a skiing trip in the Pocono Mountains. The station wagon pulled out of the church parking lot at 5:00 A.M. Immediately one of the girls asked if the rear dome light could be turned on and left on. Noting that the light would make the pre-dawn driving difficult, Mueller offered to leave it on only for a few minutes. But, speaking on behalf of all the girls, the young lady exclaimed that she had to study. Mueller was curious why they would ruin a great start to a four-day weekend by hitting the books, so he began to ask questions.

"'Do you have a test on Tuesday morning?' 'No,' they responded. 'Are you behind in your work?' 'No, we just want to get ahead.'"[9] The five girls stayed in the lodge studying most of the weekend. They enjoyed the slopes only a few times. When Mueller asked them about this strange behavior, he received insights into the minds and hearts of bridgers that were new to him.

"My conversation with them and several other teenagers since have yielded insight into how these kids were thinking: I have to study hard to get good grades so that I can be in honors classes and keep up my class rank. Colleges look at that, you know. If I can get into the *right* (not just any) college, then I will be able to graduate and go to the *right* graduate school. This will lead to the *right* job where I will be able to make lots of money. Then I will be able to get all the things I want, retire early, and enjoy life."[10]

The hard work ethic is a reality in the lives of many bridgers. But, for these bridgers, goals are not altruistic but materialistic. The pervasive influence of the media, family, and peers has told this generation that things are important, that money buys things, and thus you must work hard to make a lot of money. Note again the shifting attitudes among older bridgers in 1993 versus older boomers in 1971:[11]

	Bridgers 1993	Boomers 1971
Very important reasons for going to college:		
Get a better job	82.1%	73.8%
Make more money	75.1%	49.9%
Prepare for graduate/professional school	61.2%	34.5%
Essential or very important objectives:		
Be well off financially	74.5%	40.1%
Be successful in own business	42.6%	41.9%

The bridgers' attitude toward hard work and further education is largely tied to material benefits. Several reports indicate that education-related issues are the major concerns of the teens who are today's older bridgers. One study indicated that 75 percent of teenage bridgers were worried about getting a good education.[12] Closely related to the education issue, it seems, were economic issues. Seventy percent of the bridgers in the study were worried that the economy could get so bad that the nation might enter a depression.[13]

The bridgers may very well be a hard-working, driven generation. They indeed may seek aggressively the best educational opportunities. But their motivation, right or wrong, is money. Money buys things, and things bring happiness.

The Bridgers' Economic Forecast

The bridgers place financial needs high on their list of concerns, but their concern is not a statement of pessimism about their future. The bridgers see no "easy rides" to economic security and success. They realize that they will have to work hard to get ahead financially. But, as we just saw, this generation is willing to work hard. They are willing to make sacrifices today for security tomorrow.

Yet the bridgers are optimistic about their future because they still believe that their hard work will make a difference. And nearly half of today's teens are "very confident" that such earning prospects will become a reality.

On a similar note, 87 percent of the bridgers believe that they will have a better standard of living than their parents.[14] Only 13 percent indicated a low level of confidence in this aspect of their economic future.

What will be the consequence of these rosy future scenarios? Most of the bridgers believe that their higher standard of living and higher income levels will result in additional leisure time. Eighty-five percent of the respondents indicated that they anticipate more leisure time than their parents presently have.[15] With a good education that opens the door for a good job which pays well, the bridgers anticipate a future with more time for fun and recreation.

Things Buy Happiness

If initial attitudinal polls are accurate, the bridgers may be the most materialistic generation in our history. And why should they be otherwise? As we will see in detail in the next chapter, these young persons are growing up in an environment which preaches that things buy happiness.

The business and retail communities are well aware that young people are generously spending customers. In 1991 the teenage portion of the bridger generation was spending $95 billion and influencing the expenditure of $250 billion.[16] One writer described well how a Philadelphia-area mall became a purchasing temptation for teens:

> Come see all the beautiful and exciting merchandise we have for you. Touch it, feel it, smell it, pick it up, try it on, need it, want, pay for it with cash or without cash, now or later. It will make you happy, intelligent, accepted, loved, pretty, younger, older. . . . There is nothing haphazard here. No clocks, except those for sale, and few windows—the timeless, weather-less environment favored by casinos. There are no doors on the stores—the one thing nicer than an open door is no door at all. There are no signs on the shop windows—lest shopper's eyes be diverted from the merchandise. The colors of the mall are off-white, quiet and restrained—so the merchandise can shine. The entrance and passageways of the mall are tiled but store interiors are carpeted—people tend to walk faster on hard surfaces, slower on soft ones. The music is carefully engineered to encourage shopping—slow music boosts sales—and smells of chocolate, pizza and bread are wafted into the air chemically to stimulate the appetite. . . . [This is] a place where people follow the path of most insistence.[17]

University of Southern California demographer Richard Easterlin has monitored the values of eighteen- and nineteen-year-olds for more than twenty years. He is telling marketers that the generation I have dubbed the bridgers will be the most materialistic group he has studied. Get ready for an acquisition-minded generation, he tells them. This generation equates things with happiness, and they are determined to acquire those things literally by buying, borrowing, begging (their parents), or stealing.[18]

The bridgers will not have to wait until they reach adulthood to become significant consumers. The teenage portion of the bridger generation, as we noted earlier, spends their money (or their parents' money) with abandon.

Where are the teens getting all this money? Teenage Research Unlimited found that teenagers were receiving as much as $28.80 weekly for allowances, with most of those funds available for discretionary spending.[19] And by 1992, five million bridgers between the ages of twelve and seventeen were employed, many of them more than twenty hours per week.[20]

Many older bridgers are working by choice, not by necessity. They are experiencing "what one scholar called 'premature affluence'—the ability to finance consumer binges even as their parents are cutting back."[21]

But just earning money does not make one materialistic. Spending patterns better determine the priority of the consumers. For bridgers the picture is not too pretty. The evidence demonstrates that teenagers today use their money to buy non-necessity, sometimes frivolous items. "They buy clothing with all the well-heeled restraint of Imelda Marcos. Many have cars, which they use to go on lavish dates."[22] Perhaps equally indicative is how older bridgers *do not* use their money: "Only 10 percent of high school seniors surveyed last year said they were saving most of their earnings for college, and just 6 percent said they used most of it to help pay family living expenses."[23]

Bridgers are spending their money today for eating out, the latest-style clothes, tapes and CD's, and entertainment. Bridger girls are also more likely to use a significant portion of their funds for cosmetics.[24]

The bridger generation has not only been influenced to purchase items; they are now being told that they must have the *best* products and services. In 1968 only 7 percent of driving teenagers owned their own car. Over a third of them did in 1994. Well over half of the older bridgers own their own television, and over a fourth have their own telephone.[25]

The Bridgers and Charity

Virtually all of the bridgers' discretionary funds are used in their selfish pursuit of happiness. Only a negligible portion is directed toward the church, missions, or any charitable organization. Their spending behavior pattern is not unlike the wealthiest of families. Families with an income of $100,000 or more contributed 2.9 percent of their income to charity. This level of giving compares unfavorably with families with an income below $10,000, where the average charitable giving rate was 5.5 percent.[26]

The normative attitude of the most wealthy is "we will keep more of our wealth for ourselves." Bridgers in the "have" group act like wealthy persons, since virtually all of their money can be used for discretionary spending.

Unfortunately, this pattern of charitable giving differs little among Christian and non-Christian bridgers. The Christian bridgers are more influenced by the media, which tell them that they deserve the best, than by the words of Christ, that tell them to take up their crosses and follow Him.

The church has responded ineffectually to the cries for materialistic pleasures. With the boomers, busters, and bridgers, a typical church response has been to avoid the topic of money and stewardship lest we offend them. After all, the pundits tell us, asking for money is one of the top "turn-offs" among the unchurched.

Certainly some church leaders have addressed the issue of stewardship in ways that are offensive and sometimes unbiblical. But several churches have demonstrated that an honest and biblical approach to stewardship engenders healthy giving patterns. I observed my own pastor, David Butler of Springdale Church in Louisville, Kentucky, spend several weeks preaching stewardship. His approach was solidly biblical and challenging. Perhaps the most fascinating aspect of this emphasis was the response of bridgers in our church. For many, it was obvious that they had never heard such teachings. And they responded with excitement and generosity.

The Desire to Buy Things

We are only beginning to see the pervasive influence of materialism on the bridger generation. Quite frankly, no other generation has been pounded again and again by television, videos, radio, billboards, and numerous other media forms. And this influence has been prevalent since the bridgers' birth. They simply know no other world. The world of materialistic gain is the world they live in day-by-day, hour-by-hour.

But this dominant influence may have disastrous consequences. The bridgers are now so certain that things buy happiness that many are willing to resort to unethical and illegal activities for personal gain. We now hear on a regular basis how bridgers are willing to lie, cheat, or steal with little moral compunction. The news media tell us repeatedly of individuals who have stolen, cheated, and lied to get what they wanted. What will be the ethical standards of the bridgers whose entire lives have been influenced by the materialism of the media? The answer is frightening. A study conducted by the Pinnacle Group found that older bridgers are far more willing than business people to become involved in unethical acts for personal gain:

- Nearly *three-fourths* of the bridgers stated that they would falsify business expenses, compared to 15 percent of the business community.
- Almost six out of ten bridgers indicated that they would be willing to serve six months' probation for criminal activity to make $10 million illegally.
- Twice as many bridgers as business persons would willingly cheat to pass a certification test.
- Twice as many bridgers would lie to claim more insurance.[27]

The Materialistic Competition

I could wish that my own bridger sons were not affected by the materialistic world in which they were raised. Indeed, my wife and I have attempted to teach them the value of a Christ-centered home, relationships, and other non-materialistic concerns. But a recent event pointed up either my failures or the success of the media, or both.

Our family made a last-minute trip to the beach in Florida, since we were already nearby in southern Alabama. Since I did not have a casual pullover shirt to wear with my swimsuit, I made a quick trip to a local store to purchase one. Noticing that the item was on sale, I expected to make the purchase with pocket change. Much to my surprise, the shirt was about three times what I expected to pay. Due to my rush, I made an unwise decision and purchased the item anyway.

When I wore the shirt in front of my boys, one of my sons made a telling comment: "Hey Dad, you're finally wearing something decent. That's cool!" I would then learn that my plain white pullover shirt was "cool" because of one small mark on its front—the Nike emblem.

It is amazing how cognizant bridgers are of brand names, styles, and that which is "cool." From the day of their births, they have heard the importance of material goods, and they compete fiercely with one another to get the most.

Most bridgers will tell you that what you wear on your feet is an important status symbol. When one of my sons saw me wearing a $19.00 pair of decent-looking sneakers, he exclaimed: "Dad, please don't embarrass me by wearing that junk." I kept the shoes and let my boy suffer the indignity of his father's cheap lifestyle.

Clothing and shoe manufacturers understand the level of competition among the bridgers, the desire to keep up with the Joneses. Ron Harris describes the competitive obsession:

> What is important, youngsters say, are name brands. . . . They wear the names like badges of honor. Show up for school without them, students say, and they may be ridiculed, scorned, and sometimes ostracized by their classmates. "When people look at you and you're not wearing something that has a brand name, they'll comment on it," said Aime Lorenzo, an eleventh grader at Beach High School in Miami. "People will tease you and talk about you and say that you got no-name shoes or say you shop at K-Mart," said Darion Sawyer, ten, of Tench Tillman Elementary School in Baltimore. Children have developed divisive nicknames for non-name brands—"bobos, no-names, and fish heads. . . . ." Teasing and arguments over clothes, particularly at the elementary level, result in fights and disruptions. On the high school level, counselors report that more and more students are working, often so they can keep up their wardrobes.[28]

Reebok recently offered 175 different models of shoes in 450 color variations. Nike had 300 models with over 900 styles and colors. Shoes in the $75 to $125 price range are common, and those reaching $200 are becoming less rare. *Sports Illustrated* recognized the seriousness of the materialistic competitiveness in a cover story entitled, "Your Sneakers or Your Life."[29]

Our family recently built a new home. It is not a mansion by today's standard, but it is a nice home. As it was being built, I off-handedly commented to my family that this new edifice may be teaching them the wrong values. One son quickly commented, "Dad, you worry too much!"

I *am* worried. The world and the media have done an incredible job of teaching the bridgers that things are important. But I wonder what kind of impact I have had on my own bridger sons. They know that their parents give a tithe and beyond to the church and then to other Christian organizations. And they know that we have taught them the importance of "giving to God," as we call it in our family.

But my sons have also seen us accumulate a lot of "things." Am I sending a mixed message, at best? Or, perhaps my message is clearer than I think—a message of materialism.

A friend came to sit in my office the other day and chat. In the course of the conversation, he told me that he would be moving to another house in town. Presuming that he was "moving up," I pressed him for the location of the new house. Reluctantly, he told me the story.

"Thom, my wife and I have been concerned about the values we are communicating to Todd (their son, not his real name). We are moving to a small home away from the east side (the more affluent part of Louisville). We plan to live among, minister to, and share with people less financially blessed than we are. We're not making a big deal of it, so I would appreciate your not making a big deal of it either."

The office was quiet when he left. This man, this Christian man, saw the problem and acted upon it. Though it could be easily argued that his decision will make little difference to an entire generation, his example is one to consider. If every Christian had his attitude, what kind of difference could the church make? How *will* the church respond?

The Church Responds

Lendol Calder, a historian in New Hampshire who devoted his doctoral dissertation to American consumerism, was asked, "When did you first begin to notice the depth and breadth of consumerism in our culture?" He remembered a Christian camp that was specifically designed for college students of different nationalities. To get acquainted, the students were asked to divide into groups and to choose a song that they could sing before the whole assembly. Each group had to reach a consensus on the song.

Most of the nationalities reached a consensus and began practicing their songs within ten to fifteen minutes. But the American group debated an hour or more. Some desired contemporary music; others wanted country gospel. Still another segment sought some good traditional hymns. Finally, the Americans decided on the Coca-Cola jingle: "I'd Like to Teach the World to Sing." "The tone ringing in his ears, Lendol realized that commercial culture was what really bound these Americans—these American *Christians*—together."[30]

Rodney Clapp, in a marvelous essay in *Christianity Today*, notes the pervasive impact of consumerism on Americans today: "It is not just consumerism in its most undisguised, hackney manifestations that should concern us, but consumerism as an ethos, a character-cultivating way of life that seduces and insinuates and acclimates."[31]

Clapp considers today's consumerism antithetical to Biblical values. "This, too often, is consumption that militates against the Christian virtues of patience, contentedness, self-denial, and generosity—almost always with a velvet glove rather than an iron fist. It speaks in sweet and sexy rather than dictatorial tones, and it conquers by promises rather than threats."[32]

This ethos is the only world American bridgers know. And the world of marketers knows well that this generation is the largest group ever to view things as essential to happiness. John Naisbitt, in his *Trend Letter*, recognizes the vast consumer potential of bridgers, in an article entitled "Here Comes the Millennial Generation! How They'll Affect Marketing, Management Styles."[33]

Yet another researcher suggests that sellers of goods and services hawk their products to the bridgers now, not later: "Children age eight to twelve have over $8 billion of their own money to spend, and spend it they do—about $6 billion annually. Unlike any other consumer group, virtually all of their money is discretionary."[34] He further states that bridger children are ready to spend at unbelievably young ages: "American children begin the process of becoming consumers as early as age two, when they first accompany parents on shopping trips. By age ten, they make more that 250 purchase visits to stores each year. American young children spend the majority of their money on sweets and snacks (35%) and playthings (31%)."[35]

Does the church stand a chance against the nefarious and malignant onslaught of materialism? Can Christians withstand the rising tide of self-centeredness and the I-have-to-have-it-all mentality?

Teach Christian Bridgers Biblical Truths about Money

One place to begin is with the bridgers who are already in the church. At the earliest ages these children should be taught basic biblical principles of money and stewardship. The words of Jesus need to be learned and applied: "Do not store up for yourselves treasure on earth, where moth and rust destroy, and where thieves break in and steal. But store up for yourselves treasures in heaven, where moth and rust do not destroy, and where thieves do not break in and steal. For where your treasure is, there your heart will be also" (Matt. 6:19–21).

Another vital teaching of Jesus about money is found in Matthew 6:24: "No one can serve two masters. Either he will hate the one and love the other, or he will be devoted to the one and despise the other. You cannot serve both God and Money." The teachings of Paul provide another key message about money and "things." In 1 Timothy 6:9–10 Paul says: "People who want to get rich fall into temptation and a trap and into many foolish and harmful desires that plunge men into ruin and destruction. For the love of money is a root of all kinds of evil. Some people, eager for money, have wandered from the faith and pierced themselves with many griefs."

Churches should provide clear contemporary illustrations of how the love of money results in destruction. One well-known story begins with seven men meeting in 1928 at the Edgewater Beach Hotel in Chicago. Some reported that these men controlled more money than was in the United States Treasury. For years the print media carried stories of these men, using them as role models for young people. Within twenty-five years, however, the fate of these seven men could hardly be described as success.

- The president of the largest independent steel company, Charles Schwab, lived on borrowed money the last five years of his life and died broke.
- The greatest wheat speculator, Arthur Cutten, died abroad, bankrupt.
- The president of the New York Stock Exchange, Richard Whitney, served a term in Sing Sing Prison.
- The member of the president's cabinet, Albert Fall, was pardoned from prison so he could die at home.
- The greatest bear in Wall Street, Jesse Livermore, committed suicide.

- The president of the Bank of International Settlements, Leon Fraser, committed suicide.
- The head of the world's greatest monopoly, Ivar Drueger, committed suicide.[36]

Model a Life of Biblical Stewardship

Merely teaching about the biblical principles of money and stewardship will never reach the unchurched bridgers and, by itself, will mean little to the bridgers in the churches. This generation must see more and more Christians whose lives demonstrate faithfulness to God's Word in matters of money. A bridger will be willing to affirm scriptural teachings if he or she can see it lived out in Christians' lives.

Adult Christians in America must examine their own lifestyles to see if they conform to Scripture or to culture. We must look inward to see if our life's goals are material (How much money will I have?) or biblical (How strong will my walk with Christ be?). We must ask if our children see us keeping up with the Joneses or keeping in step with the Spirit. We must honestly determine if we possess goods, or if they possess us. We must ask what our daydreams are. The nature of our daydreams demonstrates who is our god. We must be certain that our faith and hope is in God rather than things.

I mentioned earlier my friend who has made a deliberate and conscious decision to change his lifestyle to an attempt to live as God's Word mandates. He and his wife are already living examples for bridgers (and me!) of facing this material world with biblical convictions. My uncle, Jess Keller, has been a successful attorney for over thirty years. He lives in a nice home with nice furnishings, none of which, however, could be called opulent. But he and his wife, Betty, have given away a large portion of their wealth to their church, to Christian organizations, and to people in need. They have truly discovered that they cannot out-give God. And even though they have attempted to keep their stewardship matters quiet, many know of their generosity and example.

The bridgers need more living examples such as these to see the source of true joy. They need to see Christians who live simply and give joyfully. Illustrative examples are informative; incarnate examples are convicting. C. S. Lewis said, "If I find in myself a desire which no experience in this world can satisfy, the most probable explanation is that I was made for another world."[39] The bridgers must see in Christians some lives which are obviously being lived for that other world.

CHAPTER 6

The Media Generation

Highlights

- Bridgers spend over forty hours each week watching or listening to various forms of media.
- Seventy-one percent of PG and PG–13 movies contain vulgar references to excretion, intercourse, or the genitals.
- Many of the favorite bridger rock groups have pledged allegiance to Satan.
- Pastors and priests on television are depicted as incompetent idiots or wishy-washy persons with few if any biblical values.

> *Through the miracle of TV, our children can witness war, murder, rape, hate, prejudice, sexual promiscuity, and a host of other inappropriate behaviors before they are even allowed to cross the street alone.*
>
> Walt Mueller
> *Understanting Today's Youth Culture*

My three sons were not only a key motivation for my writing this book; they were also among my most important primary sources. My middle son, Art, and I were traveling home from school on one of those rare occasions when just the two of us were in the car. Somehow we got into a discussion of this book. When I asked the question: "Art, what do you think is one of the biggest influences on your generation?" His response was quick and certain: "That's easy—the media."

His certitude surprised me, so I began to delve deeper. Why would he see the media as such a profound influence upon the bridger generation? "Think about it, Dad," he responded:

My generation usually wakes up in the morning with their radio and CDs playing the hits of today. While we get ready for school, we usually channel surf—you know me, I like to see ESPN's Sports Center. On the way to school we listen to our favorite radio station. And we may make it through the school day without television or videos, but when we get home it's channel surfing again. Except some of my friends are spending a lot of time on the Internet. We get our homework done and, for *most* of my friends [his point was clear; I do not let him or his brothers watch television during the school week], they watch a bunch of shows at night. The weekends are even heavier with television and music and rental movies or theater movies. It's media all the time!

But I reminded Art that my generation, the boomers, grew up on television as well. Indeed, we were often labeled "the television generation," since we were the first to have the tubes in our homes virtually our entire lives.

The boomers, moreover, had more than the television. We were also "the Beatles generation." I told Art that I purchased my first 45-rpm record when I was eight years old. On one side was the hit "I Want To Hold Your Hand." The flip side was "I Saw Her Standing There."

We had radio stations as well, I told Art. For me, WBAM ("The Big Bam") in Montgomery, Alabama, was the 50,000-watt station that had all the big rock 'n' roll hits of the sixties. I can still remember clearly concerts of Sonny and Cher, Herman's Hermits, the Animals, the Cyrcle, and many more.

Movies were popular for my generation too. In fact, some of the more popular movies, such as "The Graduate," both reflected and shaped the boomer generation.

But Art knew all these facts. He had heard them from me many times. His point was *not* that boomers and busters were not influenced by the media. Indeed, the generation that witnessed the assassination of John F. Kennedy and the murder of Lee Harvey Oswald still remembers clearly the visual impact of television. Art was referring to the *pervasiveness* of the media upon the bridgers through the seemingly endless options it offers. As he discussed the difference between the two generations, I made mental notes, some of which are reflected in chart 12.

Art's point was well made. The difference between the boomer and the bridger generations is not absence of media versus presence of media. The difference is the pervasive influence of media upon the bridgers with the unbelievable number of options available. The boomers were media-influenced, but the bridgers are media-dominated.

Chart 12
The Media's Influence

Boomers	Bridgers
Television:	Television:
Three to four channels	Forty to 100 channels
Primarily black and white	Mostly color
No stereo	Stereo available
Fuzzy image	Clear image
No close-captioned	Close-captioned option
No remotes	Most all have remotes
No MTV	MTV
Radio:	Radio:
Few options/stations	Numerous options/stations
LP's, 45's, and eight-tracks	CD's and cassettes
Movie Options:	Movie Options:
Go to a theater	Go to a theater
One or two movies on television	Unlimited movies on television, including movie channels
No movie rentals	Wide range of movie rentals
Computer:	Computer:
Very few had computers	Many have computers with Internet access
No Internet	

The Media Facts

Older bridgers spend more than forty hours per week watching or listening to various forms of media. Although television is still the dominant media, it accounts now for slightly less than half of all media time.

Chart 13
Older Bridgers' Time in Media
Hours Per Week[1]

Television viewing	21.8
Listening to radio	10.4
Listening to recorded music	8.9
Watching rental videos	4.5
	45.6

The younger bridgers, those who are not yet teenagers, probably will spend more time in media activities than their older peers. They already are watching more than one hour more television per week than older bridgers.[2] And though the data are still preliminary, the younger bridgers may *add* to the media mix with ten hours of time on the Internet. At this point it does not appear that other media times will decrease. Thus the younger half of the bridger generation may spend nearly *sixty hours* each week in various forms of media within the next few years.

Television Time and Facts

In 1946, the first year of the baby-boom generation, only 10,000 Americans owned televisions. Just four years later, 10.5 million sets were in American homes. And by 1960, 54 million sets were influencing the boomers and their parents.[3] According to the Nielsen Media Research group, by 1989, 92 million households owned televisions. Two-thirds of those households owned two or more sets as well as VCRs.[4] An amazing revelation reported in one study was that an average of 3.4 television sets were in households where a young adolescent lived.[5]

Today's home is built around the television set. A home builder shared with me that one of the major decisions made by new home buyers is deciding where to locate the cable-connection outlets. He also told me that it is not unusual for some new homes to have four to six outlets! The placement of sofas and chairs reflects the priority of the television in the American family.

Music Time and Facts

Chart 13 shows that bridgers love their music; indeed they listen to the radio or recorded music nearly twenty hours per week. Today 97 percent of the older bridgers will listen to the radio in a given week.[6] The weekend evenings are the most popular times, with 83 percent of the bridgers listening to FM radio.[7] Top 40/contemporary-hit radio is the most-listened-to music among teenage bridgers (see chart 14). But the bridgers are not monolithic in their preference of music styles. Over one-fourth of the generation enjoys the oldies/solid gold songs of the sixties, the music of their parents' generation.

Movies Time and Facts

Today's bridgers account for nearly one-half of all cinema ticket sales.[8] According to Teenage Research Unlimited, almost 90 percent of teenagers

Chart 14
Percentage of Teens Who Listen to the Following Formats

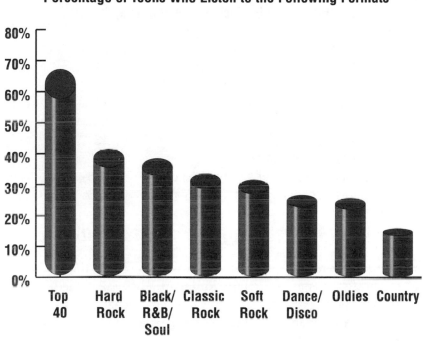

rate movie-going as an "in" thing to do; 83 percent say renting movie videos is "in" as well.[9] Additionally, in 1991 bridger teenagers watched an average of fifty-four movies on cable and broadcast television.[10]

The types of movies watched by bridgers provide interesting insight. Conservative Christian teenage bridgers were asked what type of movie they had seen in the past six months. Considering the background of these youth, the responses were disturbing:[11]

	% of Youth
G-rated movies	30%
PG-rated movies	71%
PG-13-rated movies	76%
R-rated movies	68%
NC-17-rated movies	10%

Parents of Christian bridgers can take little comfort if their children attend only PG and PG-13 films. The content of these films is often antithetical to Christian values:

Chart 15
Percentage of PG and PG-13
Movies Which Include the Following:[12]

Use of "F-word"	25%
Take the Lord's name in vain	61%
Vulgar references to excretion, intercourse, or the genitals	71%
Imply sexual intercourse	50%
Display intercourse	13%
Show explicit nudity	30%
Depict moderate or severe violence	75%
Show alcohol and/or other drug abuse	74%

Television: The Biggest Media Influence

Among the various media avenues, television is clearly the most influential on the bridger generation. The dominant advertising medium for the bridgers is television, a reality that seems unlikely to change for the next several years. But more than the advertisers, the programs themselves seem to both shape and reflect the generation.

Single-parent homes of bridgers, a growing segment, watch significantly more television than those in two-parent homes. The late afternoon has become a favorite time for television viewing for the single-parent bridgers.[13] Though only a fifth of bridger parents admit that they use the television as a baby-sitter, the viewing realities of their children suggest otherwise.[14]

The younger bridgers, those born between 1983 and 1994, watch more cable television than any other age group. These younger bridgers spend 60 percent of their viewing time with cable, versus 13 percent with network shows, and 27 percent with syndicated shows.[15]

Though the single-parent bridgers and the younger bridgers represent the largest television-viewing segment, the entire generation watches and is affected tremendously by the power of this pervasive medium. What has an entire generation of television taught our children? What are the values communicated by the medium? The answers are becoming clearer and more disturbing.

The Violence Factor

In 1992 television viewers watching the NBC network news witnessed a terrible scene of violence. The video began at a funeral in a Florida cemetery for the burial of a teenage suicide victim. The deceased girl's father appeared on the scene, distraught over his daughter's death. He began to blame his ex-wife for the girl's death. Under the camera's watchful eye, the man pulled a gun from his jacket and murdered his former wife.[16] Millions of television viewers had witnessed an actual murder.

Violence seems to boost television viewing. Thus, the networks, cable television companies, and syndicated shows increase the violent content of their programming for higher ratings and, consequently, higher advertising revenue. Noted one concerned writer: "The name of the game in television viewing is to build an audience, and violence is an effective means to gain viewers. One Fox Network executive admitted that the highest rated segments of its 'Reporters' series were the ones that featured lots of blood."[17]

Among the highest-rated news stories were those with a major theme of violence.

- Susan Smith murders her two young sons because they are inconvenient.
- Amy Fisher attempts to murder the wife of her lover.
- The Menendez brothers kill their parents to gain an immediate inheritance.
- Figure skater Nancy Kerrigan is attacked by those who feared her competitive edge.
- Lorena Bobbit slices off her husband's penis.
- O. J. Simpson is accused of murdering two persons, one of whom was his former wife.

Television violence has increased in both real-life reporting and fictional accounts. In 1955 there were no violent shows on the air during prime-time viewing. By 1965 there were six hours of violent programs. The violence content of prime-time shows increased to twenty-one hours in 1975, and twenty-seven hours in 1985.[18] Today it seems that only the threat of government intervention can stem the tide of violent television programming.

What effect does television violence have on the bridgers? It may cause them to be immune or indifferent to the horrors and tragedies of real violence. "I remember passing an automobile accident and seeing a man with his head almost completely cut off," said a Kentucky teenager. "I guess I was a little grossed out, but it didn't really bother me. I had seen a lot worse on television and the movies."[19]

Some studies indicate a direct correlation between television violence and the violent behavior of the bridgers. Dr. Brandon Centerwall found a disconcerting relationship between television and violent behavior. He does not blame television solely for violent actions, but he concludes that "if, hypothetically, television technology had never been developed, there would be 10,000 fewer homicides each year in the United States, 70,000 fewer rapes, and 700,000 fewer injurious assaults."[20] We saw in chapter 4 that the bridgers are a violent generation. Television's role, though the specifics cannot be determined with certainty, has at the very least created an environment that encourages violent behavior.

The Sex Factor

Sexual mores have changed in America. Whether television is more causative than reflective is debatable. What is not debatable is that moral values depicted on the small screen have degenerated rapidly.

1952:	*I Love Lucy Show.*	Lucy is with child but the word *pregnant* was not allowed in the script.
1961:	*The Dick Van Dyke Show.*	Rob and Laura Petrie sleep in twin beds separated by a nightstand.
1965:	*I Dream of Jeanie.*	Television censors banned the appearance of Barbara Eden's belly button.
1978:	*James At 15.*	The lead character loses his virginity.
1987:	*Cheers.*	Sam (Ted Danson) refuses to get up from a table because he has an erection.
1992:	*Civil Wars.*	Actress Muriel Hemingway appears naked with her arms blocking complete frontal nudity.
1993:	*NYPD Blue.*	A police officer has sex with a woman. A drunken policeman drops his pants anticipating sex with a prostitute. Another policeman is seen naked from the rear in the shower.[21]

Every four minutes during prime-time network television, characters display sexual behavior or talk about sex. Yet only about 1 percent of the sexual references occurs between a married couple.[22]

But the world of television sex is *not* the real world. Rarely does the small screen depict consequences to promiscuous behavior. Rarely does the television depict the poverty and brokenness of young single mothers. Rarely do the media mention sexually-transmitted diseases. Rarely does television tell us about the pain of broken relationships.

The bridgers, if they really believe the world of television sex, will see few if any problems with premarital and extramarital intercourse. Television researcher Barry Sapolsky concluded: "If an adolescent watches years of TV where people engage in flirtatious or explicit behavior, those thousands of images over the years will teach them that sex is pleasant—and without consequences."[23]

Bridgers spend more time under the influence of television than under the influence of any one person, including their father or mother. And this impersonal influence is sending a strong message about sex that will have devastating consequences for an entire generation.

Other Television Messages

Note the presuppositions behind most television shows:

1. *The traditional, biblical family is the exception rather than the rule.* A strong antifamily sentiment is ever present on the television. And even in those shows where two parents are present at home, the biblical norm is subject to scorn and ridicule. The "Murphy Brown" and Dan Quayle controversy of 1992 was but a taste of the disdain television depicts for the family. Some popular shows are almost devoted to ridiculing the traditional family: "Married with Children," "The Simpsons," and "Roseanne," to name a few.
2. *Traditional families are unsatisfactory or oppressive.* Dysfunctional family situations always work out. When traditional families are shown, they consist of two idiotic adults with disrespectful, immoral children.
3. *God and religion are unimportant.* One study of one hundred network television shows looked at 1,462 speaking characters. Of that total, 1,381 had no religion or relationship with God whatsoever.[24]
4. *Pastors and priests are not depicted as people you would care to know.* Rarely has a clergy person been depicted on television as a person of strong convictions, admirable character, and spiritual strength.

Other television messages that the bridgers are receiving: happiness is found in money and materialism; beautiful people are the norm; alcohol clears the mind; relationships should be short-term. The television is the baby-sitter and the moral guide for the bridger generation. The church has a tremendous challenge to counter such a pervasive influence.

The MTV Factor

A few of my peers suggested that the bridgers could be named "the MTV generation" because of the tremendous influence of this network upon them. Does MTV really affect this generation so profoundly? Are Christians overreacting to the impact MTV has upon bridgers? Is this music channel the instrument of Satan or merely a reflection of the bridger culture?

When it first appeared in 1981, MTV reached only 1.5 million homes. Today the network can be found on almost all basic cable packages, reaching 55 million homes in America.[25] MTV, perhaps more than any other television medium, understands the bridger generation. MTV founder and chairman Robert Pittman understands his network's impact upon this generation: "We're dealing with a culture of TV babies. They can watch, do their homework, and listen to music all at the same time."[26]

Pittman knows that this generation has a relationship with the television unlike any previous generation: "The only people who can understand the new way to use that television set are the people who grew up with it. . . . They . . . will accept almost anything on the screen."[27]

George Barna acknowledges MTV's influence on the bridger generation: "Although there is no research to confirm it, MTV has probably had as great an influence on teenagers as any other television programming. The primary influence seems to have been the channel's ability to redefine teenagers' expectations of television programming, to reshape their attention spans, to present them with new ideas about society and relationships, and to confirm the acceptability of certain perspectives and behaviors. The channel has also given life (and a platform) to new cultural icons. Madonna, Peter Gabriel and Janet Jackson are among the circle of idolized and influential performers who might not have had an audience without the push their careers received from MTV."[28]

Barna notes that kids from Christian families are just as likely to watch the network as those who do not attend church. While Barna does not defend MTV, he does not see it as the ultimate evil. "Its influence is possible only because of the vacuum in the lives of young people that is no longer filled by family, church, and school. As these three institutions have surrendered aspects of their historical responsibilities in developing young people's values, perspectives, and lifestyles, something inevitably had to emerge to fill the gap."[29]

Correlations measure *likelihood* of outcomes statistically. For example, if a community reported fifty murders in a year where forty-five of the murderers were redheads, the statistical correlation between being a redhead and being a murderer would be high. But we could not conclude that most murderers will be redheads. To say that Christian and non-Christian bridgers watch MTV with equal fervor does not mean that the program has no negative effect on the viewers. The Bible teaches that we are to fill our minds with the good and pleasing things of God (Phil. 4:8). Many would argue that MTV is inconsistent with those things God intends for us to see and hear. God's Word supersedes correlative relationships. And His Word clearly teaches that the minds of bridgers should not allow room for MTV.

The Music Factor

Bridgers love their music. The younger cohorts memorize mostly harmless words from such music kingmakers as Disney, whose "The Lion King" tunes are still on the lips of young bridgers. But by the time a bridger reaches pre- or early adolescence, an entirely new and different arsenal of music appeals to his or her senses.

In 1988 a major research project sought to discern the influence of music and media on youth. As best as I can discern, the researchers, six college professors, had no agenda to advance, but their conclusion was straightforward: "Youth . . . need the media for guidance and nurture in a society where other social institutions, such as the family and the school, do not shape the youth culture as powerfully as they once did."[30]

This simple statement is loaded with profundity. The family and the school are no longer the primary influence on this younger generation. The media, including the music industry, are to a large extent raising our kids!

But what values are being used by the music industry to raise the bridger generation? Walt Mueller conducted a study of the younger-generation music for the nineties. He acknowledged that the groups and styles are fluid. Bridger loyalty is typically short-lived. But Mueller did find several consistent themes evident in the music over a few years. These are some of the values our younger generation is being taught.[31]

Sexual Promiscuity

Numerous nineties stars could be cited to support this theme: Nench Cherry, TLC, R.E.M., Van Halen, Motley Crue, Naughty by Nature, to name a few. So many examples could be given, most of which would be inappropriate for this book. We will mention one of hundreds of possibilities here. Motley Crue's song "Slice of Your Pie" is an account of a passionate sexual encounter with a nineteen-year-old school girl. The theme in that song is consistent with other bridger hits of the nineties.

Sexual Perversion

For much of the music industry, there is an anything-goes attitude when it comes to sex. Rapper Kool G. Rap used such graphic terms to brag about his sexual deviations that they cannot be printed here. Prince and Living Colour are but two more "artists" who consistently sing and write about sexual aberrations. Indeed, it was the heavy-metal band Living Colour, in their album "Stain," that encouraged bridgers to enter the "wonderful world of bi-sexual behavior."

As one listens to the lyrics of many of the bridgers' favorite groups of the nineties, he or she senses that deviant behavior is actually normative behavior. Homosexuality, bisexuality, incest, bestiality, and abusive sex are examples of the "freedom" that the lyrics encourage. Of course, sex between two lifetime partners in marriage is rarely, if ever, depicted or encouraged.

Violence

The most violent music is heavy metal. The very names of some of the groups suggest violence. "The names of the bands like Impaler, Slayer, Napalm Death, Cadaver, Morbid Angel, Deicide, Overkill, Stormtroopers of Death, and Body Count give obvious clues to the lyrical and thematic content of their songs."[32]

When Guns n' Roses produced a video for their song "Don't Cry," they included numerous scenes of violence, "including a gun to the head, male-female fight, female-female fight, and murder by way of a car accident."[33] Mueller cites the band Malevolent Creation as a group that consistently promotes violent acts. One song, "Systematic Execution" has these lyrics: "Hot steel prods into your eyes/Executioner nods, optics spew/Tanks roll forward claiming lives/Focus on death, nothing new."

Sexual Violence

If the fifties and sixties introduced us to a genre of music for romance and love between young people, the nineties have introduced us to those relationships turning sexually violent. One of many examples in the early nineties was The Geto Boys' song "Mind of a Lunatic." This song graphically describes an angry Peeping-Tom who violently rapes a woman, slits her throat, and then proceeds to have sex with her corpse. The album that included this song sold 150,000 copies within a week of its release."

Substance Abuse

While some performers have done an admirable job in encouraging bridgers to avoid drugs, those examples are a distinct and small minority. No fewer than eight major rock stars have died from drug-related excesses in the nineties. The 1993 triple platinum album, "The Chronic" by Dr. Dre, was named after a potent strain of marijuana. It was the biggest-selling rap album to date in 1993. Al Jourgensen, lead singer in the group Ministry, makes most of his albums while high on acid. He describes himself as a "drug connoisseur."[35]

So, while many adults are fighting with fervor to counter the drugs-are-cool culture among bridgers, the music world in which the bridgers live is sending a decidedly different message. The government has invested millions of dollars to fight drugs among youth, but at least to this point, many bridgers are listening to their music instead of their parents and public authorities.

The Occult

Some bands of the nineties claim allegiance to Satan. Their songs are filled with the activities of satanic rituals. Venom, in its song "Possessed," recognizes Satan as "my master" and calls listeners to "praise him," while professing to "drink the vomit of priests." In its song "Sacrifice," this same group professes to sacrifice to its master Lucifer.

Rebellion

In adolescence there is a tendency to rebel against authorities, and the music of the bridgers certainly encourages such rebellion. Twisted Sister produced a song, "We're Not Gonna Take It," in which a son throws his father down a set of stairs and out a window. Jackyl's song "The Lumberjack" accompanied a video showing a youth sawing a school-teacher's desk down the middle with a chain saw.

Mueller notes that "a child's obsession with blatantly rebellious music should serve to tip off parents to their teenager's pain and hurt. Usually teens who are obsessed with this type of music identify with it and, in doing so, find its unhealthy messages to be a therapeutic outlet for pent-up aggression."[36] But Mueller warns that this music can affect the well-adjusted bridgers as well: "There is always the danger that this same type of music can come between well-adjusted 'normal' kids and their parents by saying that it is all right to dishonor and disobey those whom God has placed in authority over them."[37]

Hopelessness

The theme of hopelessness invades the bridger generation through different media, but particularly through their music. Axel Rose, of Guns n' Roses, exemplifies this theme in the song "Welcome to the Jungle," which tells listeners to expect to "die in the jungle."

And Nirvana, with their lead singer the late Kurt Cobain, recognized that part of the appeal of the group was its hopelessness and anger. Yet in one of his last public statements, Cobain expressed amazement at Nirvana's popularity "because I'm just as confused as most people. I don't have the answers for anything."[38]

The music of the bridgers affects more than their ears. Some music industry leaders claim their music reflects the generation's values. Perhaps that is true, but the music is also a reinforcing influence that has devastating, even deadly, consequences.

The Internet Factor

A recent article highlighted the explosive growth of Internet use: "Give up humans. Further resistance is useless. In April 1996, the Internet was available to 24 percent of persons. . . . Eight months earlier, only 16 percent had access."[39] Chart 16 depicts the rapid growth of the Internet for various purposes.[40] Most likely, by the time you read the numbers below, the usage will be significantly higher.

In 1995 my son Art knew of only one person in his class who had Internet access. One year later nearly a majority of his classmates were on-line, and he was among that group.

Years from now, pundits will be assessing the impact of the Internet upon the first generation to grow up with it. It will be the media influence television was to the boomers. What will be the evaluation of this new media?

Chart 16
Percentage of Regular On-line Users Who Use It for Various Purposes

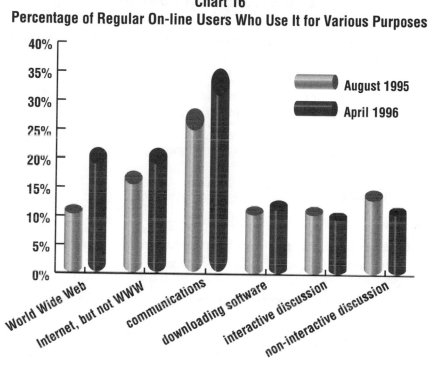

On the positive side, we will undoubtedly see the Internet as an amazing educational tool. Even today my three sons regularly "surf the net" for their reports and projects. The amount of information available is incredible.

The net is also an important interactive communications tool. Many bridgers are already entering "chat rooms" to express their opinions and insights on different issues. Though the data are preliminary and sketchy, the bridgers may very well be the most informed and responsive generation of this century because of their involvement with the Internet.

Like any medium, however, the Internet can also be a tool of destruction and evil. The level of pornographic filth available on the net is growing regularly. And it is almost impossible to monitor bridgers' use of the Internet for pornographic and other ill-founded purposes.

Another potential problem is the addictive nature of on-line access. There always seems to be "just one more piece of information" to view and absorb. Because of its interactive nature, the Internet may soon replace television as the medium of greatest addiction.

What will be the impact of the Internet on this generation? It is too early to judge, but it will be significant. Watch for this issue to be one of the utmost concerns for the bridger generation by the year 2001.

The Church Responds

The media are more than a technological influence on the bridgers. They are a way of life.

Though exceptions can be found, we must conclude that the media culture is generally doing a terrible job of raising our kids. But then again, being the parents of this generation should not be the media's job.

How can the church respond? Details will be given in chapter 11, but for now we will offer two important starting points.

Family Advocate

The church must be an advocate for the family—not the family of television and movies, but the family of Scripture. In recent years the church has spoken with timidity against the pervasive media concept of family. Perhaps we feared a "Murphy Brown" response. Perhaps we considered the situation overwhelming. Whatever our reasons, the church has been a nearly mute voice in the debate over family values.

Christians must recognize that the bridger generation is buying into the media's philosophy and values. But, we also must remember that we serve a God who honors the cries of His prophets. In our own human efforts, the move to counter the media influence is impossible. But by depending upon God's power as we speak the truth in love, we can offer the bridgers a true alternative to the culture of the media. The words of the Lord to Zerubbabel must be His words to the church today: "'Not by might nor by power, but my Spirit,' says the LORD Almighty" (Zech. 4:6).

A Relevant Voice

In addition, the church itself must be a culture to which bridgers can turn. The majority of the bridger generation sees the church as irrelevant and impotent. And those bridgers who do turn to the church often find Christians who cannot accept "those kind of people." Too many Christians refuse to leave their gospel ghettos.

Rick Warren is the pastor of Saddleback Valley Community Church in Orange County, California. This southern California church has grown to become one of the largest churches in America. Though Saddleback is not specifically targeting bridgers, it has a philosophy to reach the unchurched that is a model to reach the bridgers as well.

First, Saddleback communicates and practices love to unbelievers. Warren notes, "I know of many churches where the members love *each* other, and they have great fellowship, but the churches are still dying because all the love is focused inwardly."[41] Loving the unchurched bridgers is costly, and it makes church members leave their comfort zones.

Second, Saddleback meets needs. Perhaps the greatest perceived need of the bridgers is a place to be accepted and loved. Such acceptance at Saddleback does not mean that they condone sinful lifestyles, says Warren: "In order to love unbelievers unconditionally, people must understand the difference between acceptance and approval."[42]

Third, Saddleback provides biblical teachings that both communicate and convict. Warren understands that some of the teaching and preaching that is presented in many churches is unintelligible to both the Christian and the unbeliever. At the same time, well-communicated teaching must not compromise the biblical message. Of these churches, Warren said: "In their attempt to be relevant, these churches sacrifice biblical theology, doctrinal distinctives and the gospel of Christ. The call for repentance and commitment is compromised in order to attract a crowd."[43]

Some churches in America are providing an alternative to the pervasive media culture today. Unfortunately, these churches are few in number. Those churches that reach the bridgers in this century and into the twenty-first century will be churches of love and acceptance. But that love and acceptance will not preclude strong biblical teachings about right, wrong, truth, and godly living. Love will abound in bridger-reaching churches. But it will be a love that has the clear and distinct boundaries set forth by God in His Word.

CHAPTER 7

The Fears of the Bridgers

Highlights

- The greatest fear among the bridgers is that something bad will happen to their families.
- Bridgers fear they will not make it financially as adults.
- This generation, like no generation before, has a fear of being a crime victim.
- The bridgers admit that they do not know right from wrong.
- The bridgers live in fear of AIDS.

I can't remember not being worried about something.
Sometimes I'm happy, but most of the time I'm just worried.

"Ben"
sixteen years old, from Florida

In less than six years the number of bridgers who feel stressed out about life has increased from 25 percent to nearly 40 percent. An even higher increase has been experienced in those who fear being the victim of a crime. Bridgers as a majority fear that they will not be able to afford an education nor have a comfortable lifestyle.[1] They also live in daily fear that their homes will be turned upside down by divorce, death, or violence.

Suicide rates among persons five to fourteen years of age have tripled since 1950. In 1950 about 0.2 out of every 100,000 persons in this age group committed suicide. Today 0.7 out of 100,000 bridgers as young as five years old will commit suicide.[2]

The suicide rate for the oldest bridgers is even more dismal. In 1980 8.5 out of 100,000 teenagers ages fifteen to nineteen took their lives. By 1991 the suicide frequency among the oldest bridgers was 11.0 for every 100,000.[3]

In a strange way many bridgers see suicide as a way to control something in a world that is beyond their control. As absurd as it may seem to some people, some older bridgers today take their lives as a final statement that they exercised final control in their lives.

Most of the concerns of bridgers, however, are short-term. Few in this generation look beyond the next few months, much less years, to identify their greatest fears. This short-term perspective is explained partly by the bridgers' age. Children and adolescents of any generation rarely worry about issues that would affect the next century. But the bridgers are unique in that many of them refuse to look long-term because they have doubts about their own survival in the more distant future.

In this chapter we will look at ten major fears of the bridger generation. I have examined literally hundreds of resources about children and youth in this generation, and I have listened to hours of their conversations in different focus groups. The ten themes you are about to read were recurring themes. I have little doubt that they represent the true worries of this generation.

In addition to delineating bridger fears, I have attempted to list them in order of magnitude. That task is subjective and is an educated guess at best. Different research yields different rankings of fears. For example, one researcher found that 74 percent of older bridgers fear "one of my family getting AIDS," the fourth-ranking concern among those polled.[4] Yet another researcher found that AIDS was not a key concern of the bridgers. "In our national survey of teenagers, when asked to list the top two or three most pressing issues they are facing, AIDS was named by only 1 percent of the group!"[5] Even this researcher saw the AIDS issue to be on the minds of bridgers, though not a priority. "AIDS exists as an ever-present irritant residing in the recesses of their minds, an issue to be acknowledged and recognized, but not necessarily one that drives their moment-to-moment decision making."[6]

We thus look at the ten greatest fears of bridgers with the understanding that the relative import of each fear varies with different studies. But these fears do seem to be reflective of a generation that worries a great deal.

Fear #1: "Will Something Bad Happen to My Family?"

I remember well as a child sitting in church with my parents. Dad was rubbing my neck, and the monotone of the preacher was about to put me to sleep. All of a sudden I was wide awake with fear. I looked at Mama, then at Dad, and had this inexplicable sense of grief about the possibility of either one of them dying.

In later years I would learn that such an experience is common among children. We learn to live in a world of stability and security, and the loss of either parent shatters that serenity.

Bridgers fear changes coming to their families. But, unlike prior generations, this fear is not primarily the fear of death, but the worry of divorce and desertion.

Amy is a fourteen-year-old bridger from Florida. Her parents have been married seventeen years, but she fears that the marriage will not last. "You should hear my parents fighting. Sometimes I feel like they love each other, but then they scream and threaten to divorce. One of these days they'll probably go through with it."[7]

But why would Amy think that they would divorce after seventeen years? "That's an easy question," she responds. "About half of my friends live in broken families. Why should mine be any different?"[8] How does Amy feel about this possibility? "It scares me to death." Looking at her feet and speaking softly now, she continues, "Where would I live? Would we have enough money? Would I see both Mom and Dad? Would I have to spend time in two homes? What about my friends? Yeah, it scares me to death."[9]

We saw the disheartening statistics about the family in chapter 3. The bridgers are growing up in the midst of the highest rates of divorce. More children are living in single-parent families than ever before. That this fear is uppermost on the minds of the bridgers should be no surprise.

Let us review some of the findings of Judith Wallerstein's study of the effects of divorce on children:

- About half of the children of divorce become underachievers and worriers, and they are angry and disapproving of themselves.
- Sixty percent feel rejected by one or both parents.
- Many of the children enter adulthood with guilt and worry, and they themselves have multiple relationships and marriages that end in divorce.

Wallerstein also noted that children of divorce have problems with rebellion, depression, discipline, guilt, fear, inability to concentrate, and lack of trust.[10]

In future years we will report on the devastating impact of fatherless bridger homes. As we have seen, half of the bridgers will grow up without their father in their homes for some part of their childhood or adolescence. The fear of the fatherless home is a justified fear of bridgers. One youth expert noted: "We now know that father's absence is the greatest variable in the present and future well-being of children and teens."[11] He goes on to explain the grave consequences of fatherless homes: "Children who grow through the difficult, challenging, and formative years of adolescence without their dads have a greater risk of suffering from emotional and behavioral problems such as sexual promiscuity, premarital teen pregnancy, substance abuse, depression, suicide, lower academic performance, dropping out of school, intimacy dysfunction, divorce, and poverty."[12]

Bridgers fear the breakup of their families. Their fears are well founded.

Fear #2: "Will I Get a Good Education?"

Researchers speak with unanimity about the bridgers' view of the value of education. One study found that three-fourths of the generation feared that they would not get a good education.[13] The bridgers fear that they cannot get into college and, if they can, they worry about how they will finance their education.[14] And nearly half of the young people worry about taking the SAT or ACT exam.[15]

Barna's research found that education-related concerns were the number one worries of the older bridgers. Indeed, his data showed that the worry about education overshadowed all other concerns:[16]

Chart 17
Major Concerns of Older Bridgers

Education-related concerns	45%
Relationships	24%
Emotional pressure	17%
Physical threats, violence	13%
Financial difficulties	13%
Substance abuse	11%

Why are bridgers so concerned about education? One reason is that their parents are concerned. A significant number of the bridgers' parents interact with their children about grades and performance. Many bridgers are simply trying to please their parents and meet their expectations. Parents of bridgers are often more concerned about their kids' grades than any other aspect of their lives. This concern often engenders anxiety among the bridgers.

The bridgers are realists about the economic value of an education. They believe that a college degree is the ticket out of poverty or financial mediocrity. In 1971, 74 percent of boomers entering colleges listed "to get a better job" as an influence on their decision, and 50 percent listed their desire to make more money.[17] But as bridgers prepare for college, their motivations are different. Over 80 percent said they intend to go to college to get a better job, and three-fourths are motivated by the need to increase their earning power.[18]

Ironically, the bridgers see the value of a college degree to be less than it was in previous years. They see a flooded market with more degree-holders than ever before, and they realize that many of their peers may find little value in their education. It also seems that each bridger believes that he or she will not be among the have-nots. And the bridgers feel the competitive pressure to stay ahead of their peers.

Bridgers are worried about getting a good education. In their world of moral and family uncertainty, they think their only path to happiness may be found in the material world.

Fear #3: "Will I Be Able to Make It Financially?"

I asked my three bridger sons to tell me of their three greatest fears or worries. Of course, I had to let them know that this question was research for my book rather than the inquiries of a probing parent. Only one fear was mentioned by two of my sons; no single worry was articulated by all three. The worry mentioned by my youngest and oldest sons was the worry of their financial well-being once they are on their own.

Their responses surprised me. They have been raised in a middle-class home where they have rarely been deprived materially. Though their wish list has probably not been fulfilled, I cannot say that my sons are lacking in material needs. Where did they find this fear?

"Dad," my oldest son Sam commented, "there are no guarantees out in the world. A college degree does not mean you'll get a good job. And if you get a good job, you may not get to keep it."

Sam's words were representative of many bridgers. Over the course of several months, I spoke with numerous youth, almost all of whom fit one of the following situations:

- One of their parents was presently unemployed.
- One of their parents worked in a manufacturing or blue-collar position where the work force was being trimmed significantly.

- One of their parents held a middle-management position where downsizing was taking place.
- One of their parents had to make a recent career change.
- They knew a family well that fit any one of the above scenarios.

The bridger generation may have several labels, but one among them would have to be "the downsizing generation." These young people have grown up in a world where job security has been severely challenged. And though recent data indicate that the downsizing trend may be stabilizing, that environment has made an indelible mark on the bridgers.

Less than half of the boomers in 1971 considered the objective "to make more money" to be very important. But over three-fourths of the older bridgers feel that way.[19] Only 40 percent of the boomers had a life goal "to be very well off financially" in 1971. Three-fourths of the bridgers see this goal as essential or very important.[20] Nearly 70 percent of thirteen-year-old bridgers deemed "having a high-paying job" to be very desirable in 1995. In that same group only 52 percent felt it was important "to make a difference in the world," and a mere 42 percent deemed "being personally active in a local church" as desirable. Among the fourteen-year-olds only, 35 percent felt being in a local church should be a high priority.[21]

The bridgers are clearly worried about their economic futures. Even those in financially comfortable homes today are concerned that they will be unable to have such a lifestyle when they reach adulthood. The bridger generation may live in a material world, but they doubt their own ability to continue in that world in the future.

Fear #4: "Will I (or Someone I Know) Be a Victim of Violence or Crime?"

In the 1996 presidential elections, the stable economy engendered few concerns for the electorate. The only issue that was mentioned consistently as an issue of fear was crime. For the bridger generation, crime and violence are ever-present fears. One study showed that 75 percent of older bridgers feared that someone in their family would be a crime victim.[22]

As we noted in chapter 4, the bridgers are the most violent generation in our nation's history. They are the victims or the criminals in a growing trend of violence. In 1950 the rate of fourteen- to seventeen-year-old youths who had been arrested for a felony was four per one thousand. By 1985 the rate had increased over thirty times to 118 per 1,000. And in the four-year period from 1988 to 1992 the number of juveniles arrested for murder nearly doubled![23]

I was a baby boomer growing up in increasingly crowded public schools. I can remember the school bully demanding that we pay him a quarter or he would beat us up at recess. Yet I can still remember my having the confidence to tell the principal about the bully so something would get done.

Many bridgers in our public schools live in fear. A survey by the Centers for Disease Control concluded that one in five high school students carries a weapon to school. Among boys, one in three carries a weapon with the intention of using it if necessary.[24] The National Association of School Psychologists found that 125,000 secondary-school teachers are threatened with physical violence each school month and that 5,200 are actually physically assaulted.[25]

Mueller notes that the statistics about violent behavior among children and teens have become increasingly alarming. "The National Center for Health Statistics reports that homicide by firearms is now the second-leading cause of death (after motor-vehicle accidents) for fifteen- to nineteen-year-old whites. It is the leading cause of death for African-Americans in the age bracket."[26]

The violence portrayed in the media seems to have a paradoxical effect on the bridger generation. The ever-present scenes of violent acts and gory incidents lower the level of sensitivity to violence in the real world. Meanwhile, the deluge of violence on television and in the movies engenders a fear among bridgers that "it might happen to me."

The American Board of Family Practice has noted certain behavioral patterns growing among bridgers as a result of their fears of violence. Let us review the data from chapter 4:

- Calling home to say they have arrived somewhere safely—84 percent.
- Taking along a friend when going to an area that seems unsafe—83 percent.
- Avoiding parts of town because they seem unsafe—77 percent.
- Intentionally wearing clothes that appear less expensive—58 percent.
- Taking self-defense lessons—20 percent.
- Carrying a chemical spray such as mace—14 percent.[27]

One final note: 54 percent of the older bridgers believe that family violence is a very serious problem for them and their peers.[28] Many need not leave their homes to see and experience violence on a daily basis.

Fear #5: "Will My Friends Still Like Me If I Don't Go Along?"

Peer pressure is nothing new. Every generation faces challenges and pressures from people whom they loosely identify as friends. Paul is a fourteen-year-old bridger from Tennessee. His peers see him as a likable and friendly person. Most of them do not see Paul as one who would yield to peer pressure for wrongful acts.

"I guess I have kept my nose clean," Paul responds. "Other than some minor things, I've really never been in trouble." One of the girls in the group asks Paul if it is easy to say "no" to his friends when they try to get him to do something he knows is wrong. "Easy? Hardly. I don't like being made fun of. I don't like being called a wimp. But you know what really bothers me? I'm afraid that one day I won't say no. The pressure is just so incredible."[29]

One is more likely to yield to peer pressure when parents are not around. Often parental absence can be explained by divorce or both parents being at work. But, in many bridger families, the parents simply do not take the time to be with their kids. One study found that older bridgers spend four hours each day with peers, one hour with both parents, forty minutes with their mother, and only five minutes with their father.[30] Yet another study found that bridger teens spend an average of only thirty-five seconds a day with their father.[31]

With absent and uninvolved parents, bridgers are likely to turn to their peers for guidance and example. Unfortunately, many of their peers offer poor role models. The following chart shows just how significant peer influence is upon bridgers.[32]

Chart 18
Peer Influence upon Bridgers

Statements	Percentage Agreeing
My close friends understand me better than my parents do.	70%
I feel right now in my life I learn more from my close friends than I do from my parents.	70%
I'm more "myself" with my close friends than with my parents.	68%

But what are the specific pressures placed upon bridgers? The top five Mueller identifies are less than encouraging:

- Pressure #1: To have the perfect body.
- Pressure #2: To be dressed and groomed properly.
- Pressure #3: To be socially active.
- Pressure #4: To drink and use drugs.
- Pressure #5: To have premarital sex.[33]

Fear #6: "How Do I Tell Right from Wrong?"

One of the distinguishing features of the bridger generation is its inability to distinguish right from wrong. And many of the bridgers *know* they do not know. A study by the American Board of Family Practice found that 56 percent of female bridgers and 61 percent of male bridgers thought their generation had a serious problem because they "had no sense of right or wrong."[34]

George Barna has surveyed teenage bridger attitudes in recent years. He has shown in his research that these bridgers cannot know right from wrong because they do not believe in an absolute truth—and without absolutes, truth is relative. Relative truth means that one person's "right" may be another person's "wrong." Look again at some of the attitudes of teenager bridgers:[35]

Chart 19
Attitudes about Truth

	Agree	Disagree	Don't Know
What is right for one person in a given situation might not be right for another person in a similar situation.	91%	8%	1%
When it comes to matters of morals and ethics, truth means different things to different people; no one can be absolutely positive that they know truth.	80%	19%	1%
There is no such thing as "absolute truth;" two people could define "truth" in conflicting ways and both be correct.	72%	28%	0%

Bridgers are confused. Not only does the majority of the generation admit that they have difficulty discerning right from wrong; they also say that such concepts as right and wrong are elusive and situational. What then can we anticipate from this generation as they lead us in the twenty-first century?

Fear #7: "Where Will I Find the Time To Do Everything?"

The bridger generation may be the busiest generation in history. Educational consultant Gloria Fender explains: "Life is getting complicated. Kids are busier than ever with extracurricular activities, community involvement and responsibilities at home, especially if both parents work."[36]

Indeed, the bridgers do have more choices and more responsibilities than previous generations during childhood and adolescence. They have more choices in sports, more choices in recreation, more choices in school, and more choices in church. But the generation to this point has shown little discernment in making choices. Often they refuse to say "no" to any option; the result is often frustration and sometimes burnout.

A major problem in the bridgers' lives is the expectation that they have childhood fun while taking on adult responsibilities. One fourteen-year-old bridger explained it this way: "Mom wants me to be involved in a lot of activities at school. She wants me to take college prep courses. And of course she wants me to be involved in church. But she works a lot, so I have to clean house, cook, and baby-sit." I asked this girl how she felt right now. Her response was concise but clear: "Tired—real tired."[37]

Fear #8: "Do I Have to Have Sex This Young?"

A study of older bridgers by the American Board of Family Practice yielded some revealing if not shocking insights about today's adolescents today and sexual pressure. A full two-thirds of the girls stated that one of their greatest fears and problems is the "pressure to have sex."[38] The pressure came from different sources. Of course, the first source typically mentioned by the girls was a boyfriend or a date. But, surprisingly, other sources of pressure were almost as great.

These bridgers were perceptive enough to realize that the media, particularly certain advertisers, contributed to an ethos which says premarital sex is fun, good, and expected. Indeed, the media have convinced many parents, politicians, and educators that premarital teen sex is inevitable. These adults therefore urge "safe sex" rather than abstinence.

In several focus groups I was amazed to hear young teenage girls report on their parents' attitudes about sex. "You know, sometimes I think Mom actually wants me to be sexually active," said a Tennessee girl. "She sure doesn't do anything to discourage it. I just wish sometimes she'd give me some rules and boundaries."[39]

But sexual pressure is not limited to the female bridgers. The same study by the American Board of Family Practice indicated that 54 percent of the male bridgers named sexual pressure as one of their greatest fears. Repeatedly in focus groups I heard both boys and girls crying out for boundaries from the adult world. But most reported a dearth of such guidelines and discipline in their homes, schools, and even their churches.

The facts about bridgers and sex are not encouraging. The average age for first-time intercourse for girls is fifteen; the boys' average is fourteen.[40] Nearly three-fourths of bridgers will have sex by the time they are high school seniors.[41]

This fear of the bridger generation is well-founded. The consequences for this most sexually active young generation ever (even more than the boomers) are devastating. More than one million bridger girls become pregnant each year.[42] One study estimated that 40 percent of fourteen-year-old bridgers will become pregnant at least once before they turn twenty.[43] Almost half of these pregnancies will result in live births. About one out of ten will miscarry, and four out of ten will be aborted.[44] Since *Roe v. Wade* legalized abortion in 1973, over one fourth of all abortions have been performed on teenagers.[45] That proportion is likely to rise among the bridger generation.

The bridgers fear another consequence of premarital sex: sexually transmitted diseases (STDs). Just twenty years ago there were only four known types of STDs. Today there are over thirty.[46] Most teenage bridgers know a friend or an acquaintance who has had an STD.

The most prevalent STD among bridgers is chlamydia. The highest infection rate is among bridger girls age fifteen to nineteen.[47] Mueller notes the symptoms of this disease: "Women with chlamydia experience vaginal itching, abdominal pain, nausea, and fever, while men experience pain during urination and discharge from the penis."[48] But Mueller sees an increase in more serious consequences: "Women who are pregnant may experience problems, including infections in the baby or the death of the fetus. Chlamydia can cause sterility in both men and women."[49]

Other STDs which are ravaging the bridger generation include gonorrhea, syphilis, genital warts, herpes, and pelvic inflammatory disease. But the STD engendering the greatest fear among bridgers is AIDS. Because so many of the bridgers are terrified of AIDS, we have made that fear a separate topic in the next section.

A large number of the bridgers fear the consequences of a sexually-active life because they know the guilt and heartache which follow. They know that the media, peers, and adults who told them that premarital sex was good and OK are wrong. They know because they have experienced the pain themselves.

Mueller notes that some bridgers are attempting to fill a void in their lives through the intimacy of sex. "In an effort to fill the void that exists because of bad choice, some sexually-active teens choose to sleep around with numerous other partners. With each experience comes a deeper sense of emptiness and heartache and a greater desire to move on to another sexual relationship, all in the never-ending quest to make things right."[50]

Fear #9: "Will Someone I Know or Love Die from AIDS (Maybe Me!)?"

For the bridger generation, AIDS is not some distant problem known only through the evening news. To the contrary, the disease is ever-present in the minds of these young people. And though a cursory survey may not reveal this fear, a prolonged discussion with a bridger will typically produce some insights into his or her concerns about AIDS.

The American Board of Family Practice uncovered this fear in their recent study. Bridgers were asked about their greatest concerns for the future; five concerns were cited by approximately three-fourths of them. Among the top five was the fear of AIDS. In fact, the fear was explicitly stated as "one of my family getting AIDS."[51]

The simple phrase in the study "one of my family getting AIDS" is revealing. Not only are the bridgers fearful of AIDS for the future of their nation and world; they fear AIDS infecting someone in their *families*. Almost every bridger has knowledge of someone in their schools, churches, neighborhoods, or communities getting the dreaded disease. For this generation, AIDS is a real and present danger getting ever closer to them and their families.

We cannot know with certainty the number of bridgers who are HIV positive, but recent data indicate that the disease may have its fastest growth rate in this generation. In 1993 the number of bridgers diagnosed with AIDS increased 214 percent in just one year.[52] The rate of growth of the disease in the bridger generation is probably much higher than the 1993 number. Since it takes as long as ten years for the infection to manifest into visible symptoms, likely thousands of bridgers have contracted the disease but are unaware of it.

In the focus groups which I led, the topic of AIDS was not something that the bridgers would mention in the early parts of our conversation. Inevitably, however, as the discussion progressed, the topic would arise. It seemed as if these young people were attempting to deny the reality of a disease that could eradicate a significant portion of their generation. But their attempts at suppression were futile. Eventually the fear came to the surface.

I remember well a discussion with a seventeen-year-old bridger male who seemed extremely agitated about AIDS. "I've got this buddy that really gets around. I bet he's had sex with ten to twelve girls in the past year," the young man commented. "What are the chances that he's been infected?" he asked. "How soon before he notices something is wrong? Can he be tested now for AIDS? If he has it, how long before he dies?"[53]

Though I could admire the young man's concern for his friend, I strongly suspect that his fear was for himself. With the increase of sexual activity among the bridgers and with the increase in their number of sexual partners, this fear is probably more widespread than we had previously considered.

Fear #10: "Will I Ever Have a Happy Marriage and Family?"

The greatest fear of the bridgers concerns the stability and hope of the family into which they were born. That present fear is extrapolated into a future fear. Simply stated, a majority of bridgers do not believe they will have an intact and "good" family when they reach adulthood. And while this fear is among their greatest, one of their greatest desires for their future is a good home life. Look at some of the hopes, desires, and perspectives of the older bridgers:

- This generation, by an overwhelming majority of 73 percent, believes that children of divorced parents have more problems than children of non-divorced parents.[54]
- One of the greatest desires of older bridgers is to have one marriage partner for life.
- Most of the bridgers have a strong desire to have a spouse and children.

- Three-fourths of the bridgers believe that parents at home are the best instructors to instill values in their children.[55]
- Though both genders in significant numbers desire a strong family in their future, female bridgers particularly give this agenda a high priority.

While bridgers mention traditional family values among their greatest desires, most believe they will not see such dreams fulfilled. They fear that the deterioration of the traditional family is inevitable, and that they themselves will not be immune. As one Florida bridger shared: "I see how many families are screwed up. I see my own family and what Mom's and Dad's divorce did to me. You know, my greatest hope is to have a 'normal' family. But my greatest fear is that I won't."[56]

More than any other generation, the bridgers have been the victims of the deteriorating family in America. Many have seen firsthand the devastating consequences of the broken family. But because the problems with the family are so widespread, the bridgers are cynical about the prospects of their experiencing a good family life in the future.

The Church Responds

Fear is bad news. The gospel is *the* good news. The church has the solution to the fears of the bridgers, a solution they can find nowhere else. The church has the message of Jesus Christ. The most-frequently-mentioned prohibition in Scripture is "do not fear."

Why then has the church to this point done such an anemic job of communicating this message to a generation that would welcome such hope gladly? The bridgers fear family turmoil, lack of education, financial stress, violent crime, peer pressure, lack of discernment, lack of time, sexual pressures, AIDS, and a less-than-happy future family. The fears are many; the hopes are few. Why has the church to this point failed to be the beacon of light and harbor of hope?

Natalie is a seventeen-year-old bridger from Georgia. By her own admission she was a "worry wart" with many fears. She thought the church would have some answers. For the first time in her life, despite the fact that her parents are unchurched, she starting seeking a church. Listen to her story.

My life was a wreck. I began to understand why suicide seemed like a good idea. Some of my friends at school went to church, so I started visiting around.

I really didn't expect what I found at most of the churches. Maybe I was expecting these churches to be real strict, but they were anything but that! Most of them didn't seem any different than school. Oh, the people may have put on a Sunday smile, but after you were around them a while, they pretty much acted like my friends and their parents who aren't in church.

And most of the preaching was pathetic. The preachers either talked in a way that made no sense to me, or they were eager not to offend anybody listening. In either case it was watered-down Christianity.

After about three months of visiting around, I was ready to give up. The church really wasn't that much different than the rest of the world. But then I came to this church. The people are different. The kids are different. Everybody's friendly. The preaching is easy to understand, but it sure isn't watered-down. I can tell that the pastor cares for people, and his preaching tells it like it is from the Bible. I never before realized that the Bible had anything to do with my life today.

It wasn't long before I really began to know the difference between right and wrong. And I also knew that *I* was wrong. I know now what sin is, and I know that I am a sinner. Just two months ago I accepted Jesus. I've still got a lot of changing to do, but for the first time in my life I have hope.

Dr. Rainer, when you write this book, will you ask pastors and church members why they water down that message that I needed to hear? Will you tell them that I almost gave up on the church until I came to one that preached and taught with love and truth? Please tell them that my generation is dying to hear the message of Christ without compromise. And tell those in the church too.[57]

Yes, Natalie. And thank you. Consider it done!

CHAPTER 8

The World
They Will Know

Highlights

- The bridger generation will work and live with diverse racial and cultural groups. But this interaction may not foster a greater understanding and acceptance between the different groups.
- The bridgers may lead a sexual counterrevolution.
- We cannot predict with any degree of certainty how the world of advanced technology will impact the bridger generation.
- The bridger generation will have more "have-nots" and "haves," with fewer in the middle.
- The bridgers could be called "the isolated generation" or "the desocialized generation."

> *The young are prodding society to contemplate the future.*
> *They are, after all, the people who are supposed to carry the*
> *load for society in twenty years. . . . The ranks of the nation's*
> *youth are going to be large enough for the young to demand*
> *that society focus on their needs.*

Roper's The Public Pulse

I have mixed emotions about being a baby boomer. It is good to be one of the seventy-six million who comprise the largest generation in America's history. Collectively we, the boomers, have dictated much of the course of our society. Such influence was certainly what we demanded in the sixties.

I am not very pleased, however, with the way we have wielded our influence. In fact, I am sickened by the mark we have left on the nation. We demanded our rights, and we now have a nation that focuses inward. Not a

133

day goes by that we do not hear yet another news story about some person or group demanding their rights. The stories of altruism and sacrifice become fewer and farther between.

Mine was the generation that insisted on free love. Free love and individual rights often meant extramarital sex and unfaithful relationships; our legacy has thus been an explosive growth in the divorce rate. Free love often meant intercourse without regard to consequences, so we left a legacy of AIDS, abortion, and abandoned families. Free love meant a new, more "enlightened" morality, so we gave the nation its most immoral influence ever. What a terrible legacy we have left.

The boomer generation wanted to "have it all," to "go for all the gusto" we could get (the advertisements of our day reflected our values), and we did. But present pleasures often come at the expense of future pain. We left a legacy of families one paycheck away from bankruptcy or families with no savings. And we gave America an economy ill-prepared for the twenty-first century. Soon our nation will not have sufficient funds to pay for Social Security and Medicare.

I am among the seventy-six-million-strong generation that set a new course for the meaning of faith and absolutes. A majority of boomers rejected the "narrow-minded" morality and truth of the Bible and the Ten Commandments. We set ourselves above truth and, in essence, became our own gods. But our rise to deity has brought chaos and confusion. We now have no set standards. As in the days of Israel's judges, everyone does what is right in his or her own eyes. And everyone has different ideas of "right" and "wrong." Moral confusion is the norm. We no longer hold our leaders to high standards of character because we ourselves really have no idea how to define strong character.

When I was a child and teenager in the sixties, I had no idea upon what course our nation was headed. We have left the bridger generation a frightening legacy. Hardly a month goes by that I do not discuss with my three sons how their values are building the future. And I share with them the mistakes of my generation with the prayer and hope that they will not make those same mistakes.

In this chapter I will share with you a glimpse of the future in which the bridger generation will live. I am no prophet, nor do I have insights that are somehow divinely given. The world I am about to describe is based only upon present trajectories. This twenty-first century is based upon a course that has been set by the present-day realities. I realize that such paths can be changed by a number of factors. In fact, I hope that many will be changed.

Sometimes when I project the future course of the bridger generation into the twenty-first century, my writings appear to leave God out of the world He created. I am not though, as pessimistic about the future as this chapter may suggest. I also am a student of God's historical work in spiritual awakenings and revivals. I know that He can change the course of history. Indeed, I could point to many books on God's work in our nation today.[1]

As you read about the world the bridgers will know, therefore, read with understanding that the course is not certain. Indeed, read this chapter with the hope and prayer that God's intervention will come soon.

The Resurgence of Faith(s)

The American media has been introspective the past few years. The power brokers seem to realize that they have grossly ignored a perspective of our nation in their neglect or ridicule of religious people and movements. Television commentator Bill Moyers writes: "Something is happening in America that as a journalist I cannot ignore. Religion is breaking out everywhere. Millions of Americans have taken public their search for a clear understanding of the core principles of belief and how they can be applied to the daily experience of life."[2]

Moyers comments further that "religion is big news—a fact that was brought vividly home to me as I did research for 'Genesis: A Living Conversation,' a new series [on] PBS stations. As the journal *Theology Today* notes: 'People seem to want to talk about God. Recent novels, magazine stories and newspaper articles reflect a more serious attention to religious matters.'"[3]

Moyers notes several signs of religious interest in America today:

- *A History of God*, a scholarly book about God, has been on the best-seller list for more than a year.
- *God: A Biography* won the Pulitzer Prize.
- Franklin Graham, Billy Graham's son, appears on the cover of *Time*.
- The media report with new interest the hundreds of thousands of men attending Promise Keepers meetings. The men gather in sports stadiums to renew their commitment to God, family, and country.
- Buddhists and Roman Catholics launch dialogues to learn about each other's traditions.[4]

U.S. News and World Report ran a cover story entitled "The Faith Factor: Can Churches Cure America's Ills?" The theme of the issue was that government was not the solution to the nation's problems, so perhaps the church had the answers. Speaking specifically about a segment of the bridger generation, one article noted: "The two most reliable predictors of teenage drug avoidance: optimism about the future and regular church attendance."[5]

What does this resurgence of faith have to do with the bridger generation and its future? First, the bridger generation may be the impetus behind this newfound interest in faith. In the next chapter this thesis will be developed more; for now let us say that the bridgers are not mere spectators in this "resurgence of faith." Indeed, despite their youth, they are the shaping influence.

Second, it is more accurate to call this future world into which the bridgers are headed a resurgence of *faiths* rather than *faith*. The bridger world of the twenty-first century is not a return to a nation and time that was dominated and influenced by Christians and their values. The nation in which our bridgers will live will be a nation of co-equal religions. Toleration of all beliefs and faiths will be the accepted norm.

Moyer's optimism about "religion breaking out everywhere"[6] must be understood as referring to the various *kinds* of religions which are bursting forth on the American scene. His words are insightful: "When I first rode the New York City subway almost thirty years ago, I was impressed by the number of riders reading the Bible in Spanish. Now I am as likely to see someone reading the Koran. Islam is America's fasting growing religion. Muslims now outnumber Episcopalians and Presbyterians, and soon may outnumber Jews. Along with Muslim minarets, Buddhist retreat centers and Hindu temples now dot our religious landscape."[7]

This future scenario may be the single most important issue for the bridgers in the twenty-first century. We will delve into the subject in detail in the next chapter. For now let us recognize that the bridgers will not live in the Christian-influenced world that previous generations knew. Theirs will be the world of Roman Catholics, Protestants, Anglicans, Orthodox Christians, Jews, Muslims, New Agers, Hindus, and Buddhists. Theirs will be a pluralistic world. And ideas of exclusivity and "right" belief systems will be resisted or rejected in the name of tolerance.

The Multiracial and Multicultural World of the Bridgers

While America has never been monocultural or of one race, different groups of race, culture, and ethnicity have largely kept to themselves. I was born and raised in Bullock County, Alabama, which was and is a county with a majority of African-Americans. Still, the world in which I grew up was largely a white world. Even when my school became integrated, racial mixing beyond the classroom was the exception rather than the rule.

Though ethnic and racial groups will continue to maintain their distinct identities, the twenty-first century may well be the first time in our nation's history when all groups meet on an equal basis. The bridgers really do not know another reality. Unlike previous generations whose knowledge of other cultures has been limited, the bridgers are growing up with daily exposure to people unlike themselves. Whether it is in their schools or viewed on CNN, the bridger generation understands that no single race or culture dominates the planet.

International migration and varying fertility rates have added to the sense of racial and ethnic diversity among the bridger generation. The baby boom generation is 75 percent non-Hispanic white, but the bridgers are only 67 percent non-Hispanic white.[8] The boomers are 11 percent black, 9 percent Hispanic, and 4 percent Asian or American Indian, Eskimo, or Aleut. The bridgers are 16 percent Hispanic, 15 percent black, and 5 percent Asian or American Indian, Eskimo, or Aleut.[9]

More of the bridgers are of mixed race than any previous American generation. A 1990 Census Bureau report stated that two million bridgers were "of a different race than one or both of their parents."[10] Susan Mitchell notes: "The largest group is children of black and white parents, but close behind are children of white and Asian parents. That translates into about one mixed-race child for every 35 members of the next baby boom [the bridgers], or about one in every school classroom."[11]

There is far more interaction between people of different races among the bridgers than any previous generation. "The oldest half of the original boomers was born into a fully-segregated society, with separate schools, neighborhoods, and public facilities for whites and blacks. The next baby boom is the product of a more integrated society."[12]

Will this racial and cultural interaction lead to greater acceptance of different colors and backgrounds among the bridger generation? The forecasts are mixed. While one might presume that more interaction leads to more understanding, we cannot make such conclusions at this point.

Mitchell notes: "While increased diversity might lead to greater racial tolerance, other signs point to further polarization among the races."[13] Her research has found signs of both acceptance and prejudice among the bridger generation. "Schools were successfully integrated decades ago, but many neighborhoods are as firmly segregated as ever. Race-related violence and organized racial hate groups are increasingly visible, and schools around the country report increased racial tension among students."[14]

We can say with certainty that the bridger generation will live and work with diverse racial and cultural groups. But we are far less certain that this interaction will foster a greater understanding and acceptance between the different groups.

More Non-traditional Families Than Any Other Generation

Ozzie and Harriet Nelson's family and the Cleaver family have been the subject of ridicule the past several years. Both television families of old have been portrayed by family authorities as "unrealistic," "unattainable," or "just plain ridiculous." The critics point out that their world was not the real world in the fifties and sixties, and it certainly is not the real world today.

Perhaps the Nelsons and Cleavers were a bit too happy and problem-free for reality. Perhaps it is a bit much to expect the stay-at-home mother to be beautifully dressed with perfectly-applied make-up any hour of the day. But the critics are missing the point when they note these characteristics of the fictional families.

The Nelsons and the Cleavers *were* a reflection of the American family in several key areas:

- The parents were married and had no previous marriages.
- The children were biological offspring of both parents.
- Divorce was not an option.
- The fathers worked.
- The mothers stayed at home to care for children and to do household chores.
- The parents were heterosexuals, living in monogamous sexual relationships.

Whether the critics agree or disagree with the characteristics of the Nelsons and Cleavers, the families mirrored the majority of families when the shows aired. As late as 1970, 85 percent of children under age eighteen lived with two parents, and 12 percent lived with only one parent. Within just two decades, only 71 percent of children had two parents present, and 27 percent lived with a single parent.[15]

Indeed, we already have reviewed a plethora of difficult facts and statistics about the family in chapter 3. The problem with bridger families has been the dominating issue of this generation. In addition to all the data cited about heterosexual parents, a small but growing trend is the number of homosexual parents. Not only will we watch to see if the numbers increase significantly; we also will be interested to discern attitudes about homosexual parents. Recent surveys indicate a greater acceptance of these non-traditional scenarios.

How do present realities project into the future in which the bridgers will live? Barring divine intervention or unforeseen major societal shifts, bridger families will look radically different from the Cleavers and Nelsons. Compared to previous generations, the bridger generation should have *significantly more*:

- Single-parent families
- Families with a step-parent
- Families without a father at home
- Families with both parents working
- Grandparent-raised children
- Families with a never-married mother
- Homosexual parents[16]

A Sexual Counterrevolution?

Though data are inconclusive as this book goes to press, there are indications that the bridger generation may reject the complete sexual freedom advocated by the boomers. The bridger children have already seen the devastation of divorce, often caused by lack of commitment and sexual infidelity. Three-fourths of older bridgers believe that it is too easy to get a divorce. Over 70 percent believe that most divorced persons did not try hard enough to save their marriages.[17] And nearly three-fourths of bridgers recognize that "kids of divorced parents have more problems than kids with non-divorced parents."[18]

Another reason for a sexual counterrevolution is the bridgers' awareness of the consequences of unmarried sex. Over half (55 percent) of bridger teenage girls say that the "fear of pregnancy" is a very serious problem for teenagers today.[19] But nearly three-fourths of all teens fear "one of my family getting AIDS."[20]

The bridger generation is responding in two ways in this sexual counterrevolution. The first, "safe sex," is really not that counterrevolutionary, but we must recognize its advocacy among teenage bridgers.

Every twenty-one seconds, a fifteen- to nineteen-year-old bridger female loses her virginity.[21] Many are responding to their fears of the consequences of sexual activity by using contraception. Over three-fourths of sexually-active bridgers used some form of contraception in their last encounter.[22] Condoms are the most frequently-used birth control among bridgers; slightly less than half used them in their most recent sexual encounters.[23]

The second response and the heart of the sexual counterrevolution is the advocacy and practice of abstinence among teenage bridgers. Here is one good example of the church responding positively to a frightening trend among our youth. "True Love Waits" is a program which began among Southern Baptist churches, but TLW has spread rapidly within and beyond the denomination. A teen makes a commitment to God and his or her church to remain abstinent until marriage. Cards are signed and account-ability is encouraged. Hundreds of thousands of bridgers have made this commitment, and their numbers are growing.

Another trend, perhaps surprising, is that more public school teachers who teach sex education are advocating abstinence. Look at the results of this study of sex education teachers conducted by the Alan Guttmacher Institute:

- The majority (61 percent) of the teachers are females.
- Almost one-half of the teachers have fifteen or more years' teaching experience.
- Most (86 percent) teach that abstinence is the best approach to prevent sexually-transmitted diseases.
- Most (87 percent) talk to the students about the negative consequences of sexual intercourse.
- Four out of five actually provide counseling on how to resist peer pressure.
- Four out of five also teach the teens how to say "no" to a boyfriend or girlfriend.[24]

While the data are yet to be deemed conclusive, the trends are positive. The bridgers may lead our nation in a sexual counterrevolution that affirms abstinence outside of marriage and sexual fidelity within marriage.

The Unknown World of Advanced Technology

One thing is certain about the twenty-first century: it will be much more technologically advanced than it is today. But we cannot know the specifics of the advance.

As recently as 1994, "the Internet was the playground [primarily] of university scholars, graduate students, and computer experts. Research institutions and the federal government picked up much of the tab of maintaining the system. Advertising and the search for profits were verboten."[25] Now millions of persons enter the Internet for the first time each year. And the graphics part of the Internet, the World Wide Web, is becoming more and more a useful marketing medium.

The world the bridgers will know in the twenty-first century will be advanced technologically beyond our imagination. Trend forecasters have been woefully inept in foreseeing the nature of the changes in the past; such forecasting will be even more difficult in the future. We know that the rate of change will increase. We do not know how the bridger generation will cope with the pace of change.

The oldest bridger will be forty-eight years old in 2025; the youngest will be thirty-one. Edward Cornish, editor of *The Futurist* magazine, made ninety-two predictions for developments by 2025. He called the world in 2025 "the cyber future" but cautioned that even futurists cannot know the future with certainty. "Our task . . . will be to set forth a series of anticipations for the cyber society that is now developing," he stated.[26] But there is no certainty in his projections. "These possible future developments are, in the author's judgment, likely or at least plausible, based on current trends."[27]

Some of Cornish's predictions are fascinating. Some seem outrageous. Some are downright scary. We looked at some of these predictions in chapter 2; now let's look at a few more:

- A chip implanted somewhere in our bodies might serve as a combination credit card, driver's license, personal diary, and you name it.[28]
- As the global culture grows, local cultures will decline. Hundreds of languages will disappear.[29]
- The infomedia will tend to desocialize people, making them more prone to antisocial and criminal behavior.[30]
- Skills and knowledge will become obsolete faster than ever.[31]
- Criminals will use cyberspace increasingly to commit thefts and escape punishment.[32]
- Electronic gambling will probably become a major social problem in the years ahead.[33]
- People's attention may become the world's most precious resource.[34]
- Cybersex systems may become widely available, perhaps early in the twenty-first century. . . . One approach involves the development of

attractive, life-like robots able to function as lovers. . . . Cybersex could become a major growth industry."[35]

- People will have car offices as well as home offices.[36]

The bridger generation will thus live in a world that looks quite different from our world today. How and where will the bridgers lead us?

New Economic Alignments

How will wealth be distributed in the twenty-first century? Economists and demographers disagree, but they agree that today's economic alignments will change significantly in the years ahead. Susan Mitchell notes the rising poverty rate among bridgers despite increasing governmental assistance: "For the next baby boom . . . the years of their birth have coincided with steadily increasing poverty among children, with rates rising from 16 percent in 1977 to 23 percent in 1993."[37] The results, she says, will be an exacerbation of the division between "the haves and have-nots."[38] A disproportionate number of the have-nots will continue to be black. We have already seen that in 1993, 18 percent of white children were poor, but 46 percent of black children lived in poverty.[39]

Despite the gap between black and white poverty rates, there are signs that the economic gap between blacks and whites is decreasing. Black-owned businesses grew 46 percent between 1987 and 1992, nearly twice the rate of growth for all U.S. firms.[40] While income levels remain disparate—average household income of $34,079 for whites in 1994 and $20,998 for blacks—African-American households "were the only racial or ethnic group experiencing real income gains between 1993 and 1994."[41]

One of the more remarkable stories to watch in the bridgers' future will be the rise of a black middle class. Trends point toward this phenomenon solidifying by the time all bridgers reach adulthood. Slightly under two million African-American households have a median income of $44,987, an amount that clearly qualifies as middle-class income.[42] Outside the South the median income of middle-class blacks is almost equal to the income of middle-class whites.[43]

Businesses are recognizing the growing economic power of middle-class blacks. African-American consumers have a $1 billion a day spending power.[44] "Cadillac once had an unwritten policy of not selling to blacks; today it's a leader in the automotive industry in 'diversity marketing.' Time

Warner is developing *Savoy* magazine, which it describes as a 'black *Vanity Fair.*' And *Forbes* is launching a black history magazine."[45]

The economic world the bridgers will know in the twenty-first century will not be the white-dominated world of their youth. African-Americans and other minorities will continue to see significant economic growth.

Globalization Continued

Globalization has been a trend for years. Only since the bridger generation was born have we seen that future projection begin to become a present reality. What has transpired in the last few years to accelerate globalization?

Technology is making the global village a reality, particularly among the young and educated. Indeed, the bridgers will bring to the twenty-first century the first generation to grow up truly connected to the rest of the world. The bridgers will be the first generation comfortable with international telephone calling, faxing information abroad, or communicating beyond the Western hemisphere via the Internet.

One researcher notes that the concept of "the global citizen, a term that has been reserved to globetrotting diplomats, corporate executives, novelists and athletes,"[46] is ever expanding. The bridger generation will be America's first global generation.

According to trend predictor John Naisbitt, the bridger generation will be in the midst of these megashifts:

- From nation-state to business state via the inevitable loosening of government trade controls.
- From bureaucracy to entrepreneurism through new global networks.
- From passivity to interactivity as business and governments form new alliances.
- From status quo to flexibility with new and more creative trade agreements.
- From being there literally to being there virtually which means "physical location becomes virtually irrelevant."[47]

Edward Cornish projects major twenty-first century changes related to a new global culture. This culture "will develop as infotech ties the world's people together."[48] But Cornish also notes that "the rate of global change—technical, social, and cultural—will continue to accelerate, creating innumerable surprises and dangers."[49]

The world the bridgers will know will be vastly different from the world we know today. Because of globalization, the level of change may be comparable to the change that has taken place from the Middle Ages to the end of the twentieth century.

An Age of Isolation and Desocialization

Television was the boomers' antisocial monster. Now the bridgers are growing up with television, rented videos, computer games, and the Internet.

The bridgers also have grown up in the era of time pressures. They have seen their parents pulled apart by career, family, and personal needs. Indeed, as we noted in an earlier chapter, the bridgers themselves have felt these time pressures even in their youth.

Now staying at home has become the norm for stressed-out bridgers and their families. Nearly six out of ten families today say they often bring take-out meals home.[50] Television is absorbing increasing amounts of leisure time. The home computer has become a tool for work and play. Increased Internet usage has enhanced this search for fun without associating with other people.

What are the consequences of this self-imposed home isolation? Surprisingly, new studies indicate that the isolation is more than isolation from acquaintances and casual relationships—it is also isolation from good friends as well. When asked how many friends they had seen in the past two weeks, the surveyed Americans' response was an average of 4.0 in 1994. In 1983 the response was an average number of 5.4 friends, over a 20 percent decrease in contacts in one decade.[51]

Today's solitary environment of many Americans could mean that twenty-first century bridgers will live among people deprived of social interaction. Cornish notes: "In the days before television and computers, face-to-face conversation was the primary means of entertainment, pursued around the dinner table at home" and other social avenues.[52] Cornish concludes that the increasing isolation of persons is leading to antisocial behavior: "This social entertainment trained people to deal with other people, to respect their interests, and to use them skillfully to meet one's own needs. The rise of the electronic entertainment seems to have been accompanied by increasing rudeness."[53]

Will the bridger generation live in a world of isolation and desocialization? Cornish thinks so: "If electronic entertainment continues to gain, we may become a non-society—a poorly integrated mass of electronic hermits, unable to work well together because we no longer play together. Institutions such as the family, community, church, and nation will face the challenge of seeking support from people whose loyalty is almost entirely to themselves."[54]

The Bridgers: Shaping Society's Issues

I have attended four seminars about the baby boomers. I have read at least eight books about the baby boomers. And I have lost count of the number of articles I have read about my generation. Frankly, I am tired of hearing about the baby boomers.

One baby boomer put it this way: "The great thing about being a baby boomer is that you're always at a trendy age. Whatever is on the minds of all those extra people born from 1946 to 1964 is necessarily also on the mind of anybody else who wants to sell to them or get their votes. And as all the world knows, what's on the boomers' minds is themselves and their riveting encounters with the routine phases of life."[55]

Indeed, we boomers have received a lot of attention. But get ready to abdicate the throne, boomers—the bridgers are coming! The political candidates and the hawkers of goods and services will soon discover this generation that is nearly as large as the first baby boom. The bridger generation will be the people who set and shape society's agenda in the twenty-first century.

Perhaps the most important issue of the future world the bridgers will know will be the bridgers themselves. Even now, trend watchers are commenting about them (though no one else is yet to call them "bridgers"). John Naisbitt notes: "A group of some 72 million Americans [are] coming of age. They're the so-called millennial generation, a new baby boom of persons born from 1977 to 1994. . . . Most of the new boomers will be filling schools for years to come. The millennials made up about 28 percent of the U.S. population, nearly as large as the 1946–1964 baby boom."[56]

Like the boomers, the bridgers will tend to be preoccupied with themselves. Already the demographers are touting their size and power. "Their place in the record books is already secure," comments Susan Mitchell. "They may one day surpass their parents to become the largest and most influential generation in U.S. history."[57] Make way for the bridgers. Their day in the sun is but a few years away.

The Church Responds

A few years ago, the evangelical church awakened to the crisis of teenage pregnancy and premarital sex among youth. Instead of whining about these out-of-control teens, some Christian leaders decided to be proactive. Out of this desire came the successful ministry "True Love Waits." Hundreds of thousands of bridgers have been spared the heartache and even deadly consequences of premarital sex.

Other church leaders like pastor Charles Roesel of the First Baptist Church of Leesburg, Flordia, led their churches to develop ministries for unwed pregnant woman and girls.

Though we cannot know with certainty what the future holds, we do know who holds the future. Too many churches look at the plight of our society and simply decry the degenerate world in which we live. But speaking against what is wrong is not enough. We must also act.

A few years ago I met with the pastor of a church with one of the most dynamic crisis pregnancy ministries I have ever seen. I asked the pastor about the ministry's origins, and he told me the story.

Before opening the crisis pregnancy ministries, the pastor had been outspoken against abortion. He preached against it and spoke against it in every forum possible. One Sunday morning a young lady waited quietly in the foyer of his church. After the last person was greeted by the pastor at the conclusion of the service, the sixteen-year-old girl approached him.

"I have heard your sermons and cries against abortion," she quietly told the pastor. "And I agree with everything you have said. Now I have just one question: What will you do about it?" The girl began to cry. "I am pregnant. I have no money. My parents have disowned me. My boyfriend has left town. I don't want an abortion, but can you tell me what to do? Can you help me?"

From that one conversation, the pastor led the church to start a crisis pregnancy center. They help with medical costs. They will assist in finding adoptive parents if the woman desires. They provide a home if the woman has no place to go. And they are available to be there with the women in the labor and delivery room.

Perhaps the evangelical church has done a credible job of speaking against what is wrong. As we move into a new century, we should continue to sound the prophetic voice. But we must do more than speak.

If the family disintegrates, we must provide ministries for those who fall through the safety net. If a sexual revolution continues, our Christian youth must lead a counter revolution. If the world changes too rapidly, the church must provide a haven of constancy and certainty. If people become more isolated, we must provide a community, even if those who come in are not like us.

The world which the bridgers will know will be very different from the world we know today. But even in that new world, the church needs to be a harbor of safety for those who seek to escape the storms that rage. And Jesus Christ still needs to be seen clearly through both our words and deeds.

CHAPTER 9

The Faith(s) of the Bridgers

Highlights

- The bridgers are a very religious group, but almost any religion will do.
- This generation will resist the truth that Christ is the only way of salvation.
- The "big no" of the bridger generation is religious intolerance.
- The great heresy of the Christian church in the twenty-first century will be inclusivism.

> *At this moment between two centuries, as one millennium gives way to another, we Americans must debate what it means to be a nation. We must decide our identity as a people. How are we to write a new story for ourselves unless we learn to be open about our deepest religious beliefs with people not like us?*
>
> Bill Moyers
>
> *How can I hold my truth to be the truth when so many others see truth so differently?*
>
> Bill Moyers
>
> *I am the way and the truth and the life. No one comes to the Father except through me.*
>
> Jesus Christ
> (John 14:6)

Everything I heard from Lisa to this point was impressive. With twelve other teenagers sitting in the room listening, she cogently articulated how she lived her life morally and ethically as a follower of Christ. She seemed completely unashamed to describe her commitment to Jesus, and the implications of that commitment.

Then, John asked her, "Lisa, how would you witness to Mark? What would you say to him?" I quickly learned that Mark was a devout Mormon in their class at school. "Oh," Lisa responded, "I wouldn't begin to impose my beliefs on him. He is such a good Mormon."

Now it was my turn. I tried to speak without exasperation. "Lisa, are you saying that you wouldn't tell Mark that he would have to accept Christ to go to heaven?"

Both her face and her words spoke with certainty: "Of course not; we can't be that narrow-minded and intolerant."[1]

I guess I should not have been surprised by Lisa's religiosity or her tolerance. The bridgers have learned their lessons well. The first lesson they learned is that they do not want their lives to turn out like their boomer parents. Many of them, therefore, honestly seek a God who can fill the voids in their lives.

But they also have learned well the world of political correctness from the boomer generation. The political correctness convictions of that confused generation insist that we cannot be so intolerant as to either believe or impose a single belief system. Thus the bridger generation is truly a seeking generation, but their search rarely ends with the one God who is the only way.

The PBS series "Genesis" premiered in October 1996, with a celebrated promotion called "The Resurgence of Faith." The host, Bill Moyers, asked this question before beginning the series: "Can a pluralistic America avoid the bitter fruits of religion—intolerance, ignorance and murderous fanaticism—that have occurred throughout history when faith is used as a wedge to drive people apart?"[2] Then Moyers asked the question that is fast becoming the question of the bridger generation: "How can I hold *my* truth to be *the* truth when so many others see truth so differently?"[3]

Such is the world of faith in which bridgers have been raised. It is a world that finally has room for God, but refuses to define God in precise terms. Martha Williamson, executive producer of CBS's "Touched by an Angel," expressed this view of God well: "I think the show's success lies in the fact that God is an inclusive God. God exists and wants to be part of all our lives—if we let him."[4] Pam Janis further explains this perspective of God: "The God of pop culture is not necessarily a Judeo-Christian God. He (or she) can be any form of love and power."[5]

The bridger generation has adopted this view of God. Even many bridgers in evangelical churches refuse to limit their understanding of God to the One who has been revealed in Jesus Christ. When we speak of the bridgers' religion, we cannot speak of their faith. For the vast majority we can describe it best as the *faiths* of the bridgers.

A Very Religious Group

History may remember the bridger generation as the most religious group America has ever known. Their generation is being raised in a time when the Gallup Organization reports that religion is playing a more important role in the lives of Americans (see chart 20).[6] Public confidence in both organized religion and the clergy has been renewed, despite the moral failures of many church leaders.[7] Church attendance has held steady for most age groups, but is increasing among the bridger generation.[8] Moyers writes: "We shouldn't be surprised by all this stirring. It's a confusing time, marked by social and moral ambivalence and, for many, economic insecurity. People yearn for spiritual certainty and collective self-confidence."[9]

But Moyers' ideas about "spiritual certainty" are anything but certain. He celebrates "the resurgence of religion in America, and the arrival on our

Chart 20
Percentage of Americans Who Say
the Influence of Religion Is Increasing

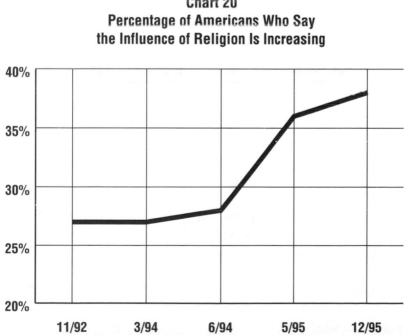

shores of so many believers of different faiths."[10] For him the different views do not bring confusion but hope. The bridgers seem to be catching that same pluralistic fever. What you believe is less important than that you believe something.

The world of the bridgers is not the world of the religion of their parents. We boomers, whether we attended church or not, saw our choices clearly. The Baptist, Methodist, Presbyterian, or some other denominational church was our choice in the neighborhood. Most of us did not see our options in Muslim minarets, Hindu temples, or New Age seances. Though Christians (in name) still dominate the religious landscape, chart 21 shows that the religious mosaic is changing.[11]

Chart 21
Estimated Members in Select Religions in North America
(in millions)

	1990	1995
Protestants	126.3	133.0
Roman Catholics	95.2	100.3
Anglicans	7.2	7.5
Orthodox Christians	5.9	6.2
Jews	7.1	5.9
Muslims	5.2	5.5
New Age religionists	1.3	1.4
Hindus	1.1	1.3
Buddhists	0.4	0.6

The bridgers are the first generation of Americans to be raised without the cultural presumption that they would become Christians or explore Christianity.[12] Many of the bridgers take a smorgasbord approach to religion. They take the elements of each religion that make them most comfortable. They may even call themselves "Christians," but the term is used generically.[13]

Do these characteristics mean that bridgers are not religious? To the contrary, they are more religious than the boomers ever were. But we cannot make religion synonymous with Christianity. The former has some general type of belief in God (or gods) that may have many expressions. The latter believes only in God as revealed in the person of Jesus Christ. The former is "tolerant" and open to many faiths. The latter is "narrow minded" and sees only one way to God.

How Many Roads Lead to Heaven?

In the next section we will look briefly at four perspectives of God: universalism, pluralism, inclusivism, and exclusivism. Universalism means that everyone is going to heaven. Exclusivism means that only those with an explicit faith in Jesus Christ will go to heaven. Pluralism and inclusivism lie somewhere between these perspectives.

Bridgers, under the influence of their loosely-religious boomer parents, rarely hold to the biblical position of exclusivism. Half of older bridgers believe that the faith one embraces is of no consequence since all faiths teach similar lessons.[14] Two-thirds of the bridgers hold to some kind of works salvation.[15] Half of them also believe that all good people go to heaven, regardless of their relationship to Jesus Christ.[16]

The bridgers also have little understanding of sin. Many believe that the concept of sin itself is outdated.[17] And 45 percent believe that Jesus was a sinner while He was on earth.[18] Without an understanding of sin, one cannot see the need for a Savior. And without the need for a Savior, we can make God into whatever image fits best. Small wonder the bridgers are confused about faith!

Where did the bridgers learn their lessons about faith? For the most part, from their boomer parents they inherited an environment of moral relativism and a world void of absolutes. An exclusive God who says there is no other way to salvation and heaven simply does not fit in this I'm-okay-you're-okay climate.

Redefining Christianity

Most bridgers still call themselves Christians.[19] But they rarely use the word in its biblical meaning of one who has a personal relationship with Jesus Christ. Look at some of the beliefs of older bridgers that contradict their Christian label.[20]

- Less than one-half (42 percent) believe that their faith makes a difference in their lives.
- Only 40 percent of the bridgers believe that God is all-knowing and all-powerful.
- Over one-half (55 percent) believe that when people of different faiths pray to their gods, they are really praying to the same God.

- Only one-third of the older bridgers believe that when they die they will go to heaven because they have accepted Jesus Christ as their Savior and have repented of their sins.

Remember, this group is the same group of surveyed bridgers who, by an overwhelming 86 percent, call themselves Christians.

The bridger generation is being influenced by adults in America, the great majority of whom do not believe that any one faith system has absolute claims on truth. What is more disturbing is that this pervasive thinking often emanates from the Christian community itself. Let us briefly look at the four positions we mentioned earlier.

Universalism

Universalism is "the belief that no human being will ultimately be lost. Sooner or later, universalists believe, God will eventually save every person."[21] Many scholars have cited the works of John Hick to defend this position.[22] In most of Hick's writings, he would be more accurately described as an advocate of pluralism, which we will discuss shortly. But he began to sound more like a universalist as he became convinced that a loving God would never exclude anyone from heaven or salvation.

The love of God is one of the key arguments universalists use to defend their position. How could a loving God allow anyone to go to hell? Or, if they deny the existence of hell, how could a loving God exclude anyone from heaven? Universalists give little attention to the sinfulness of human nature and little attention to the justice of God.

Universalists and pluralists profess concern for tolerance. They consider those who believe "Jesus is the only way to be narrow-minded and prejudiced against other religions. How dare one group claim that their way is the only way? Wilfred Cantrell Smith writes, "Exclusivism [the belief that Christ is the only way of salvation] strikes more and more Christians as immoral."[23] Joseph Runzo attacks the exclusivistic position as "neither tolerable nor any longer intellectually honest in the contemporary knowledge of others' faiths."[24]

Yet another point that universalists use is that of geographic and cultural conditioning. Ronald H. Nash, an exclusivist, states the universalists' argument: "People born in New Delhi, India, can hardly be blamed for becoming Hindus any more than someone born in Cisco, Texas, can be faulted for becoming a Baptist. If any of us had been born in Japan or China . . . it is unlikely that we would have become Christians."[25]

Universalism is not often advocated by those who called themselves Christians, but it is a belief that is growing in America. Many bridgers have been exposed to universalism and have been attracted to it.

But many bridgers have rejected universalism because of its all-embracing posture. The bridgers might affirm the salvation of a "good" Muslim, Hindu, Buddhist, Mormon, or Jehovah's Witness. And they may affirm the salvation of "good" persons with humanitarian and charitable feats, regardless of their religious beliefs. But most have difficulty including Hitler, Manson, Stalin, rapists, child molesters, and mad bombers in the universalistic embrace of God's love. That too, they argue, would be unfair.

The greatest influences upon the bridgers have been the two positions called pluralism and inclusivism. Each of these positions allows for the love of God to reach to Christians, while not being limited to Christians. Yet each of these positions can reject the salvific hope for an Adolph Hitler or Charles Manson. Let us look at each perspective briefly.

Pluralism

Pluralism holds that humans may be saved or go to heaven through numerous religious traditions and saviors. John Hick, the often-cited pluralist, explains his understanding of pluralism this way: "There is not merely one way but a plurality of ways of salvation or liberation . . . taking place in different ways within the contexts of all the great religious traditions."[26]

Most pluralists, however, do not desire to treat all religious beliefs and systems equally. They have some nebulous type of evaluative criteria for each religion. They look at each religious system according to its "goodness" or the "goodness" of its leader or leaders. Thus some religions clearly fail the "goodness" test, such as the Peoples' Temple of Jim Jones, the Branch Davidians led by David Koresh, and religions that practice human sacrifice or cannibalism.

But the Koreshes and Jones are clear examples of "bad" leaders in "bad" religions. Pluralists have difficulty drawing a clearly-defined line that separates the "good" religions from the "bad" religions. Nash notes that "pluralists have not identified a criterion to mark the line between authentic and inauthentic 'responses to the Transcendent' clearly enough to make it work on a broad scale."[27] The Koreshes and Jones are on the "bad" side of the scale, but "even though Hick tells us that Jim Jones was on the wrong side of the line, it will not be clear to everyone how to apply the same criterion in other cases."[28]

Different pluralists have different perspectives on Christianity. Most express difficulty with both the claim of the deity of Christ and the uniqueness of salvation through Him. Hick writes, "If Jesus was literally God incarnate, and if it is by his death alone that men can be saved, and by their response to him that they can appropriate that salvation, then the only doorway to eternal life is Christian faith. It would follow from this that the large majority of the human race so far have not been saved."[29]

The "narrow way" of Christ is offensive to most pluralists. They refuse to believe that other "good" religions are excluded from the salvific love of God. Whereas Christians see everyone as sinful and undeserving of salvation, pluralists measure relative goodness to determine who indeed merits the love of God.

Most bridgers today are pluralists. Like Lisa at the beginning of this chapter, they see some type of co-equality among different religions. This generation has been raised in an environment where toleration and understanding mean seeing everyone as qualitatively the same. Religions must neatly fit within this all-are-equal mentality. For Christians to claim uniqueness for their faith is tantamount to prejudice and bigotry.

Mike sat quietly as Lisa expressed her feelings about the goodness of Mark, the Mormon mentioned earlier. Because Mike was a friend of Mark's, he felt like he could remain silent no more. "Look," he said, "I know Mark better than anybody here. In all of my life I have never known a better person. If I want to find out the right and moral position on something, I go to Mark." Mike paused for a moment and then resumed speaking. "Why do we have to argue about which religion is best? Most all of them are good. Why can't we just all get along?"

The bridger generation as a majority will reject the unique claims of Christians and of Jesus Christ Himself. When Christians begin to explain to the bridgers the fallacies of other faiths, we will be judged as intolerant. Like Mike, they will want to know why we cannot all "just get along."

Inclusivism

The most dangerous doctrinal aberration facing the church in the twenty-first century will be inclusivism. This belief attempts to capture the much-desired tolerance of pluralism while affirming the redemptive work of Jesus Christ. Ronald Nash writes, "Inclusivists agree with pluralists that God's salvation is not restricted to the relatively few people who hear the gospel and believe in Jesus Christ. Inclusivists agree with exclusivists that God's universally accessible salvation is nonetheless grounded on the person of Jesus Christ and his redemptive work."[30]

Inclusivism is enticingly tempting to Christians and churches that do not want to appear narrow-minded, yet desire to affirm the work of Christ for redemption. They can proclaim that Christ is the only way, while acknowledging that others may come to Christ in their own religions. A "good Buddhist" can therefore go to heaven. That Buddhist, though unaware that Christ was the redemptive work in his or her faith, will be saved on the basis of Christ's atoning work. He or she does not "accept Christ." He or she, however, comes to Christ "anonymously" in the Buddhist religion.

Another great appeal of inclusivism is that it widens the way of salvation for those millions who die without hearing the gospel. Inclusivists insist that it is only fair that everyone has a chance to be saved. John Sanders, an inclusivist, explains "that God, in grace, grants every individual a genuine opportunity to participate in the redemptive work of the Lord Jesus, that no human being is excluded from the possibility of benefiting from salvific grace."[31]

Clark Pinnock has been one of the more dominant voices in advocating inclusivism. Pinnock is often treated as an evangelical though his views are nothing short of heretical. He has been given a welcome forum with the Evangelical Theological Society and often publishes with evangelical publishers. At least implicitly, the evangelical embrace of Pinnock conveys to many that his views deserve serious consideration.

What then are the views of Clark Pinnock? We must acknowledge that he affirms "the uniqueness and finality of Jesus Christ."[32] He would further regard "as heretical any attempt to reduce or water down this conviction."[33] But Pinnock does not believe that *explicit* faith in Jesus Christ is mandatory. Persons may be saved by the redemptive work of Christ without ever acknowledging Him or even being aware of Him.

Pinnock would therefore observe that "some intend the same reality Christians intend when they believe in God as personal, good, knowing, kind, strong, etc."[34] He would thus further state that "If people in Ghana speak of the transcendent God as the shining one, as unchangeable as a rock, as all-wise and all-loving, how can anyone conclude otherwise than that they intend to acknowledge the true God as we do?"[35] Pinnock then writes, "We must not conclude, just because we know a person to be a Buddhist, that his or her heart is not seeking God."[36] He concludes, "What God really cares about is faith and not theology, trust, and not orthodoxy."[37]

Why is inclusivism such a dangerous belief system for bridgers? First, it is heretical. It presumes that many outside of explicit faith in Christ will be saved. It allows the church to feel comfortable with other religions while millions die and go to hell.

Second, its teachings are gaining popularity in many churches, including evangelical churches. Nash notes, "The number of evangelicals who are sympathetic to inclusivism may be larger than many think. . . . My own observation of evangelical leaders in places of denominational or missions leadership along with professors at mainstream evangelical colleges and seminaries points to a number higher than 50 percent."[38] Such misguided leaders will thus affirm bridgers in their pluralistic and inclusivistic beliefs.

Third, while pluralism may be the most popular belief system among the bridger generation, inclusivism will be a desirable alternative for many. Some bridgers have a level of reverence, respect for, and hope in Jesus Christ. Inclusivism will allow them to embrace other religions while still claiming the label of Christian.

Exclusivism

Nash defines Christian exclusivism "as the belief that (1) Jesus Christ is the *only* Savior, and (2) explicit faith in Jesus Christ is necessary for salvation."[39] The first portion of the definition contrasts with pluralism, where many ways to God are accepted. The second portion contrasts with inclusivism because explicit faith in Christ is necessary. Nash notes that "Christian exclusivists begin by believing that the tenets of one religion—in this case, Christianity—are true and that any religious beliefs that are logically incompatible with those tenets are false."[40]

Though many passages of Scripture could be cited to support the exclusivistic position, two texts from the Gospel of John state the position clearly. The first is found in John 3:16–18: "For God so loved the world that he gave his one and only Son, that whoever believes in him shall not perish but have eternal life. For God did not send his Son into the world to condemn the world, but to save the world through him. Whoever believes in him is not condemned, but whoever does not believe stands condemned already because he has not believed in the name of God's one and only Son."

Jesus himself states in this text that He is the only way of salvation. Furthermore, He clearly says that those who do not believe in Him are already condemned. And from a clear reading of the text, one hears Jesus say that *explicit* faith in Him is required. There is no sense of an "anonymous Christ" in these words.

Yet another teaching on exclusivity comes again from Jesus where He affirms with clarity, "I am the way and the truth and the life. No one comes to the Father except through me" (John 14:6). Neither of these passages leaves room for pluralism or inclusivism.

But, according to our research, only about four percent of the older bridgers affirm the exclusive claims of Christ.[41] Why is nearly an entire generation rejecting a claim that has been accepted for nearly two thousand years? What is so offensive about Christ being the only way of salvation? To that response we now turn.

The Big No: Intolerance

John Hick accuses Christians who hold to the exclusivistic perspective of "validating centuries of anti-Semitism, the colonial exploitation of Christian Europe of what we call the Third World, and the subordination of women within a strongly patriarchal religious system."[42] Now, few bridgers are likely to relate the issue of intolerance to the specifics cited by Hick. Large numbers of the bridger generation, however, will see exclusivism as narrow-minded and bigoted.

No American generation in history has been confronted with the politically-correct demands the bridgers are experiencing. Major among the politically correct issues is the issue of intolerance. Toleration is seen as a virtue. Indeed, tolerant people may very well exhibit many positive characteristics.

But toleration as a virtue has limits. In an obviously extreme example, suppose a thief comes into our home demanding that we turn over our money and valuables. Unless the thief has some type of weapon to back his or her demand, should we tolerate this behavior and, with an open mind, surrender everything to the burglar?

Obviously everyone will draw the line in toleration at some point. But in our pluralistic society, an almost open-ended toleration is demanded of all faiths. Many claim that Christians in particular should not be dogmatic and rigid in their beliefs. They should be receptive to other belief systems, even if those faiths clearly contradict Christian teachings. Ironically, Christians are often called intolerant, but those who demand tolerant behavior are often the least tolerant toward Christians. Nash responds, "To assault people in such a personal way without justification is itself a moral failure; it is certainly more serious than wrongly accusing someone of defending a weak argument."[43]

Bill Moyers has become a popular spokesperson for the politically-correct-tolerance movement in religion. Moyers finds the most extreme example of intolerance in religion and implicitly includes the extreme groups such as Branch Davidians, with exclusivistic evangelicals.[44]

Such is the world in which bridgers are growing up. They are culturally conditioned and pressured by society's norm to accept with "open-mindedness" the beliefs of other faiths. To claim that *your* Savior is the *only* Savior is the epitome of intolerance. Bridgers are learning that most sins are situational and relative. But if this generation has a sin that approximates the unpardonable sin, it would be the sin of tolerance. Moyers asks, "How are we to write a new story for ourselves unless we learn to be open about our deepest religious beliefs with people not like us?"[45] For the bridgers, open-ended religious tolerance is in; "rigid" Christian exclusivity is out.

The Practice of Their Beliefs

What are the consequences of making intolerances the Big No? Though the connection between their beliefs and behavior may not be obvious to bridgers, the evidence is nevertheless clear: (1) Tolerance means that we must be open to other beliefs. (2) Other beliefs will contradict our Christian beliefs at numerous points. (3) To accept those contradictory beliefs, we must compromise our own beliefs. (4) If we compromise *some* of our beliefs, the slippery slope may cause us to compromise *any* or *all* of our beliefs. (5) We thus are left with no absolutes or standards by which to guide our behavior.

This logic has serious consequences for behavior. Over nine out of ten bridgers hold to a situational ethic: "What is right for one person in a given situation might not be right for another person in a similar situation."[46] Eight out of ten bridgers believe that no one can be certain what is morally right or wrong.[47] And 72 percent of this generation say that "truth" can never be clearly defined.[48] Is it little wonder that nearly 60 percent of an entire generation believe lying is a necessary behavior in life?[49]

Even more devastating are the attitudes and actions of bridgers who claim to be born-again Christians. Their lifestyles are hardly different from their non-Christian peers. Look at some of Barna's comparisons between the two groups:[50]

Chart 22
Moral Behaviors and Attitudes of Bridgers

	Born Again Christians	Non-Christian
Watched a pornographic movie	32%	41%
Cheated on an exam	29%	27%
Had sexual intercourse	23%	29%
Stole money or property	6%	7%
Used illegal drugs	4%	11%
Attempted suicide	3%	7%
Believes lying is sometimes necessary	45%	63%
Believes morality depends upon the situation	92%	90%

These statistics indicate that my generation, the boomers, have failed to create an environment in which our bridger children can see a clear difference between right and wrong. Our religious relativism has led to moral relativism.

Barna notes that million of our young people "want to follow Jesus and are doing their best to follow the advice and example provided by the Christians who are guiding their spiritual development."[51] But the problem is "the reliability of their mentors. When the disciplers provide spiritual noise rather than a means of discerning the true voice and calling of God, the Church is in dire straits."[52]

I recently talked with a professor who teachers busters and bridgers in a Christian school. His philosophy of teaching is to present all religious views as equal, without imposing the clear boundaries of the Christian faith. Within a few minutes our conversation had shifted to family, and he began sharing with me openly the problems he was having with his seventeen-year-old bridger son. Though no parent is guaranteed trouble-free life when raising children, I wondered if his son's problems might relate to the father's teaching on tolerance. Without absolutes we have no clear guidelines. Without clear guidelines, moral chaos is sure to follow.

The Church Responds

No one likes to be called intolerant. The word connotes a non-thinking narrow-mindedness that is determined to hurt all people except those who are like us. The secular media have begun describing evangelical churches and parachurch movements who hold clear biblical moral beliefs as "right-wing religious extremists." *Fundamentalist* is another word often used in its most pejorative sense to categorize these same groups. This world which lauds toleration of all beliefs and quickly condemns a set of fixed values is the only one the bridger generation has known.

The twenty-first century church faces a great temptation. In an attempt to appease a growing number of voices in the bridger generation, many churches, in the name of tolerance, will be tempted to water down the foundational doctrine of Christian exclusivity. Some churches will accept that other belief systems provide equal paths to God. Such will be the main heresy of the next century.

The faithful churches, however, will resist this broad path of salvation. At the risk of ridicule and possible persecution, some churches will stand firm for the true gospel.

With loving firmness, the churches that reach bridgers in the next century will confront people like Lisa, whom we met at the beginning of this chapter. Those churches will teach Lisa that to reject Christ as the *only* way of salvation amounts to rejecting Christ altogether. If we reject exclusivity, we have called the Savior a liar, since He made such claims for Himself (John 14:6).

More "open-minded" churches may attract bigger crowds, at least for a season. But those churches will accomplish nothing more than that. In their attempts to be culturally relevant, they will have become biblically irrelevant.

The churches that reach the bridgers in the next century will not compromise the exclusive claims of Jesus Christ. Their doctrinal "narrow-mindedness" will not be presented with an unloving attitude. They will speak the truth in love. And only in these churches will bridgers become disciples of Jesus Christ.

The Church Responds:
Now, Not Later

Highlights

- Over 80 percent of Christians say they accepted Christ at age nineteen or earlier.
- Seventy-one percent of Christians say they accepted Christ at age fifteen or younger.
- At present trends, we will reach only 4 percent of the bridgers for Christ.
- The most common reason churches are not intentionally evangelistic toward the bridger generation is ignorance.
- If the church does not attempt to evangelize the bridgers now, we may lose most of this generation.

> *And whoever welcomes a little child like this in my name welcomes me.*
>
> Jesus Christ
> (Matthew 18:5)

My wife Jo and I had just fallen asleep. The time was shortly before midnight on July 8, 1996. Our two older sons, Sam and Art, were on a mission trip to South Dakota. The telephone rang, abruptly awakening us. Though neither Jo nor I said a word, it was clear we both had the same thought. Had something happened to one of the boys?

Tragedy had indeed struck, but it was not our boys. It was Art's dear friend, fourteen-year-old David Brown. His sister Sarah called to let us know that David had been in an automobile accident and was surviving only by the life-support machines. He died shortly after the telephone call.

Sleep would not come for some time. I could hear myself saying the words, but they were too unbelievable to absorb: David is dead. That smile, that laughter, that kid who just delighted in life . . . gone.

Shortly after the funeral, a young man named Dave Wood experienced a sleepless night as well. David Brown and his family were on his heart and mind. He kept thinking about David being in heaven and what he was experiencing. Dave Wood began writing words. And those words reflected the heavenly experiences of young David Brown. Read the words he penned.

Insights from a Fourteen-Year-Old

Named David Brown and His Best Friend Jesus
Today I walked with Jesus,
Down the streets of purest gold;
He looked at me with eyes of mercy,
Stretched out His hands and said, Behold.

I saw the nail scars of the One
Who is Lord of Lords and King of Kings.
Then He wrapped them around me
And angels began to sing.

Mom, Dad, He is everything you promised me,
So much more than words can describe;
His love is an overflowing river,
And for all eternity we will abide.

And did I mention the buildings?
This Carpenter has style.
But Jesus just overheard me and said,
David, my greatest work is your smile.

Mom, Dad, heaven is so awesome.
There is beauty in every place,
But the greatest sight in paradise
Is the glory on Jesus face.

Still, I know its hard on you
For all of us to be apart.

But soon well be together
Because weve asked Jesus into our heart.

How thankful I am for the day
I bowed my head and prayed to receive;
I asked the Lord to forgive my sins,
And accepted the gift of Calvary.
So wipe those tears away,
And please try not to cry.
I am still your little boy, Mom.
And Dad, I am the apple of your eye.

I miss you my brother Jonathan,
Those long talks on the trampoline.
But youre gonna love it here,
Sights and sounds like youve never seen!

Only one thing could make heaven sweeter,
And thats to be with all my friends
So if you dont know my Redeemer,
Trust Him now and be born again.

Cause one day well stand before Him
When our life on earth is done.
Well want to know that Christ is in our heart,
That the battles been truly won.

Oh, theres one more great thing about heaven,
And Im going to tell it to you.
Everything Ive been taught about God, His Word, and eternity
is true!

You see, Dave Wood could write these words about David Brown because David had accepted Christ and had the promise of heaven's eternal life. In the midst of their grief, Davids parents, Mal and Esther Brown, could still rest in the assurance that they would see their son again.

The vast majority of bridgers today have not accepted Christ. In a recent and informal survey of 211 bridgers, only 4 percent responded that they were born-again Christians who had trusted in Christ alone for salvation.[1] In comparison with other generations, two-thirds of builders indicated they were Christians, as well as one-third of boomers and 15 percent of busters.[2] According to present trends, we are about to lose eternally the second largest generation in America's history.

The Urgency of the Moment

In a survey of approximately 1,300 Christians of various backgrounds and regions, I asked them at what age they accepted Christ. The responses were amazing.[3]

Chart 23
Age That You Became a Christian

Before age 6	6%
Ages 6–9	24%
Ages 10–12	26%
Ages 13–15	15%
Ages 16–19	10%
Ages 20 and over	19%

Over 80 percent of the respondents said they had become a Christian before they turned twenty years old. And 71 percent said that they had accepted Christ before the age of 15. George Barna's research seems to affirm my surveys. He comments that "one of the most significant discoveries from our research among all age groups of the population has been that most people make their lifelong, faith-shaping choices when they are young."[4]

My survey was especially concerned about all of the teen years, so the question asked specific ages up to nineteen. Barna researched the specific ages up to age eighteen and found that "if a person is ever going to become a Christian, the chances are that he or she will do so before reaching the age of 18."[5] Whereas 81 percent of our respondents became Christians before age nineteen, Barna found that "three quarters of all people who have consciously, intentionally, and personally chosen to embrace Jesus Christ as their Savior did so before their eighteenth birthday."[6]

My research and Barna's research are very close in their conclusions. Over three-fourths of persons become Christians before they turn twenty years old. Not many churches, unfortunately, are paying much attention to this reality.

Bridgers and Receptivity

A key missiological tenet is the principle of receptivity. C. Peter Wagner defines this principle by stating that "at a given point in time certain people groups, families, and individuals will be more receptive to the message of the Gospel than others."[7] Wagner finds biblical justification for the principle of receptivity in what he calls "the harvest principle." We are to focus our resources on places and people where the greatest number will come to Christ. The Savior Himself, says Wagner, indicated this mandate when he spoke to his disciples: "Open your eyes and look at the fields! They are ripe for the harvest" (John 4:35).[8]

For Wagner, common sense dictates that Christians and churches should focus their resources of time, people, and money where there is greatest receptivity to the gospel. "Although God can and does intervene and indicate otherwise, it only makes good sense to direct the bulk of available resources to the areas where the greatest number are likely to become disciples of Christ."[9]

Jesus said, "The harvest truly is plentiful but the workers are few. Ask the Lord of the harvest, therefore, to send out workers into his harvest field"

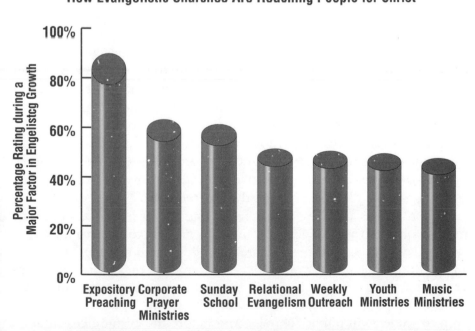

Chart 24
How Evangelistic Churches Are Reaching People for Christ

(Matt. 9:37–38). Wagner views this as a clear mandate for a heavy alloca-
tion of resources when the harvest is ripe.[10] In Matthew 10:11–14, Jesus
instructed the disciples to test the receptivity of a town. If the disciples were
not received by the townspeople, they were to leave that place and shake
the dust from their feet. "Shaking off dust," says Wagner, "was a culturally-
recognized sign of protest, in this case protesting resistance to the gospel."[11]

For decades the principle of receptivity has been advocated to reach people groups, families, tribes, and other racially or culturally tied groups. But
the most receptive group in America may very well be an age-related group.
More than any other factor—race, class, culture, etc.—age seems to be the
key to receptivity.

Barna insists that "it is helpful to recognize that not only do many people
make their life-changing decisions before they even reach high school, but
also that such a compressed time period has such major consequences."[12]
Indeed, if we look at the age frame from six through fourteen, over 70 percent of persons will have made decisions for Christ. "In other words," says
Barna, "by the time students enter high school, the odds of accepting Christ
as Savior are radically reduced; by the time they graduate from high school,
the odds are stacked against such a choice to a staggering degree."[13]

Evangelistic Churches Target Children and Youth

In a massive research project of evangelistic churches in America, my
research team and I found that many churches that had experienced conversion growth had specifically targeted people below the age of twenty.[14]
Out of hundreds of possible evangelistic methodologies, specific evangelization of youth and children was the sixth-highest rated methodology.[15]

One pastor who responded to our study was rather frank about the
declining evangelistic effectiveness of churches to the youth in America. He
said that we must reach out to those who are most receptive to the gospel.
"Ninety-five percent of those who get saved are below the age of eighteen.
It's time to get busy in the business of evangelism that works. We need quality youth pastors! We have dropped the ball too long."[16]

Many of the evangelistic churches in our study placed a significant
emphasis on youth and children's *evangelism*, not just youth *programs*. Both
staff and lay leaders sought ways to reach children and teenagers for Christ
in everything they did. A youth lock-in, then, becomes more than a fun
evening for the teenagers. The Christian youth are encouraged and motivated to bring their unchurched friends with them. Open invitations are
given to students in public schools. And before the evening concludes, a

motivational speaker presents clearly a plan of salvation. Youth evangelism is highly intentional in these evangelistic churches.[17]

We are losing the bridger generation because the efforts of many of our churches are anemic. Why have churches failed to recognize this potential harvest? Or, if they recognize the possibilities, why have they failed to respond? In my travels that take me to about forty states each year, I have listened to hundreds of church leaders. Their responses are both fascinating and frightening.

Obstacles in the Churches to Evangelizing the Bridgers

Have you noticed when Christian authors start publishing books on reaching different generations? Whether the book is about the boomers or the busters, we typically receive their insights *after the generations become adults*. And as our data tragically depict, we have lost the generation by that time.

Again, look at our estimates of the number of persons reached for Christ in each generation:

Chart 25
Estimated Proportion of Each Generation Reached for Christ

Generation	Percentage Reached for Christ
Builders	65%
Boomers	35%
Busters	15%
Bridgers	4%*

*Based on present trends among older bridgers.

We are losing an entire generation. Where is the church? Look at some of the reasons we have discerned among the hundreds of churches we have studied.

Ignorance

By far the simplest explanation for the churches that have not reached the bridgers is ignorance, or lack of awareness. Many church leaders simply do not realize that they are losing a generation. A number of them have youth ministers and active youth and children's programs. But the activities and programs often disguise the churches' failures to reach the bridgers.

One interview I conducted with a layperson in a 400-attendance church is typical. The gentleman is an active, well-meaning Christian who heads the youth committee of the church. When I asked him how many children and youth were being reached for Christ, his response was revealing.

"I'm not sure exactly how many," he responded, "but it has to be a lot. Our young people are always involved in activities, programs, and mission trips." With obvious pride he continued, "On a given week we will have as many as 75–100 children and youth involved in church activities. We have to be really reaching a lot of kids."

I later checked the church records. The prior year two persons under age twenty had been baptized.

We often confuse *activities* for *evangelism*. And while these activities may be well-intended and even serve some good purposes, they cannot replace true intentional evangelism.

"They Don't Pay Their Way."

One of the more pathetic, yet all-too-common responses to a lack of bridger evangelism is the decision not to reach out to them since they provide little income for the church.

A few church leaders were honest enough to admit that they made a conscious decision not to reach young persons since "they cost more than they give." Most church leaders were more indirect, but their intentions were still clear. In financial bottom-line issues, bridgers will not pay back in the short-term. But may God have mercy on the churches that look at people only as financial investments.

"They Mess Up the Church."

Most bridgers are different than church-going adults, partly because they come from a different generation. They do not always view the facilities of the church in the same reverent manner as the adults do. I have heard dozens of Christians express reluctance about receiving the bridgers into their churches because of the rambunctious behavior of these younger people. While destruction of property should not be tolerated, many Christians are more concerned about a scuffed floor than an eternal soul.

"They're Not Like Us."

Not only are most bridgers different because of their age; they also come from a different culture than that of previous generations. From a religious perspective, this generation is the first not using Christianity as their starting point in their search of God.

As a reminder, let us look at a few of the issues unique to this generation that we have seen throughout this book.

- They reject absolute truths.
- They are the first (as a majority) to be raised by day care instead of mother's care.
- They are the first significantly fatherless generation.
- They are stressed out about finances, sex, school, crime, and AIDS.
- They are truly the first computer generation.
- They have been influenced immensely by MTV and other media.

These are but a few of the numerous traits of millions of bridgers. If they come into our churches, they may not act like a boomer or builder adult who has been in church for thirty or more years. Will we accept them? Sadly, many churches have already answered "no."

"They Cause Too Much Change."

The churches that reach the bridgers in the twenty-first century cannot be comfortable with the status quo. Essential doctrines must not change. Biblical stands on moral issues must not change. But much that takes place in many churches will have to change to reach the bridgers.

I recently spoke in a church that asked me to recommend to them a prospective youth minister. After careful thought and prayer, I called them with the name of one of the most dynamic youth ministers I have known. The young man was especially gifted in evangelizing children and youth.

He told me that, from his perspective, the interview with the youth committee went well, but much to his surprise, he received a decline letter within only four days.

Several weeks later, I had an opportunity to talk with a member of that youth committee. She explained to me that they were very impressed with the young man. "But," she said, "when he started talking about some of his ideas and plans to reach young people, we really got worried. Our people could never accept some of the changes he would bring. We're like a happy family, and we didn't want to mess with a good thing."

The young man eventually went to another church that accepted some of the changes he and the bridgers brought to the church. In one three-month period, they reached over forty young people for Christ. The status-quo church, I suppose, continues in its comfort while eternal lives are at stake.

"But We'll Neglect the Adults."

Over the past two years I have been leading a seminar around the country on evangelistic church growth. I have been blessed to have hundreds of leaders from different churches attend and interact with me. Toward the end of my seminar, I present data on the bridgers. And I also urge church leaders to reach out to this generation *now*, while most of the bridgers are under the age of twenty.

In most of the seminars, someone will voice an objection to my pleading. "If we allocate more resources to reach these young people, we'll neglect evangelizing adults. I just can't buy that," some have said. Indeed, in a world of finite resources, choices must be made. But, according to all the research we have available, the bridgers are most likely to respond to the gospel. While we should never neglect the evangelization of adults, we must use our God-given wisdom to discern where receptivity is greatest.

"They're Too Young to Understand."

Some churches have neglected the evangelization of children and youth because of a misperception that these young people cannot understand biblical truths about the gospel. We cannot be dogmatic about a particular age at which a child can understand such basic concepts as sin, faith, and the person of Christ. But some churches act like a person must have deep theological comprehension, an attitude which disqualifies most young people. Salvation in Christ comes through child-like faith. I would think that the great majority of the bridger generation is able to understand the essential truths of the gospel.

Will the Bridgers Come to Our Churches?

Though the Christian church in America has failed to reach out to the bridgers in significant numbers, the bridgers continue their search for truth and meaning. And that search often brings them back to our churches.

Even today, half of all bridgers attend a church worship service each week. The older the bridger, the less likely is his or her involvement in church. Most bridgers pray during a given week. One-third of them participate in a Christian youth group during the week. One out of four is active in a Bible study group. And nearly 40 percent of the bridgers are involved regularly in Sunday School.[18]

These young people are involved in churches at a much higher level than older generations. Yet, if our surveys are close to accurate, only a small number of the bridgers are making decisions for Christ. What can churches do to make a difference in the lives of these young people? What can we do to make an eternal difference?

Effective Evangelistic Churches: Reaching a Generation for Christ

In my study of 576 evangelistic churches in America, I took particular interest in those churches that were successfully reaching young people for Christ.[19] In follow-up interviews with pastors, staff persons, and lay leaders in these churches, four clear characteristics emerged. We will look at them in detail in the next chapter. For now let us look at them briefly with an understanding that urgency is our central theme in this chapter.

Unconditional Love

A teenage bridger at the church I attend sometimes stays close to me before and after worship services. For whatever reasons, perhaps because I am the father of three sons, he likes being around me. His own father left him and his mother several years ago. He has no siblings, and he hungers for male leadership and love.

His story can be repeated millions of times in this generation. Theirs is the generation of broken families, fatherless homes, and abusive environments. Millions of bridgers are starved for love.

I am convinced that the single key factor in these churches' success at reaching this generation is an intentional decision to love these kids unconditionally. And without exception in the interviews I conducted, the pastor modeled that love for the congregation. Where a youth minister was on staff, the love was also modeled in him or her. As we will see in the next chapter, this unconditional love attracts the bridgers like a magnet.

Clear Boundaries

Unconditional love does not rule out having clear boundaries and discipline for these young people. In fact, in the effective evangelistic churches we studied, firm guidelines for the youth were a norm. The bridger generation has grown weary of growing up in an adult world that does not know right from wrong. Indeed, one study indicated that six out of ten bridgers felt "having no sense of right and wrong" was a major problem for their generation.[20]

One outstanding church youth program is at Springdale Church in Louisville, Kentucky, where Tracy Turner serves as youth pastor. My three bridger sons are in the Springdale youth program. One of my sons recently was involved in a prank where kids in the youth program were bombarding each others' homes late at night with toilet tissue and eggs.

My son's name came up as a perpetrator, to which he readily confessed. Tracy got my son and his friends together and read them the riot act! They spent most of a day cleaning the houses they had attacked. I then followed with a week's at-home detention for my mischievous child.

Tracy does not hesitate to let the kids know right from wrong, and he expects them to stay within those guidelines. Yet the kids love him. They respect him because he first loves them, and because he is willing to demonstrate tough love.

The bridger generation is desperate for clear boundaries. Many of them are not receiving this discipline at home, but they respond well to churches that offer guidelines from a foundation of love.

High Expectations

Closely related to the issue of boundaries is the matter of high expectations. A clear message from the focus groups we conducted was the bridgers' desire to be challenged and given an opportunity to respond.

Jason is a fifteen-year-old bridger from Georgia. His words are representative of many conversations we heard. "I'm sick of being looked down on as stupid," Jason said. "My school dumbs-down everything so we can all pass. My parents let me get away with murder. And even my church is more interested in entertaining me than teaching me."[21]

Several of us in the Billy Graham School of Missions, Evangelism, and Church Growth are involved in a comprehensive research project about churches that are reaching and assimilating people. Though our project has just begun, earlier research indicates that high-expectation churches are more successful at reaching and keeping young people.[22] High-expectation churches also will reach more bridgers in the twenty-first century.

Cultural Sensitivity

We must also affirm that churches must make some changes to reach the bridgers without compromising biblical truths and essentials. With an urgency that recognizes eternal consequences, we must seek ways to communicate with this new culture without abandoning our biblical distinctives. Some suggestions will be made in the final chapter. For now, let us acknowledge that we have to live with the tension that the apostle Paul expressed in his letters. He told the Corinthian church that, though we live in the world, we must live differently from the world (2 Cor. 10:4). Yet he also expressed the urgent need to make cultural adjustments to reach the lost: "I have become all things to all men so that by all possible means I might save some" (1 Cor. 9:22).

Bridgers need churches that can live with that tension between cultural sensitivity and biblical faithfulness.

The Time Is Now

Our research is fallible. We may reach considerably more than 4 percent of the bridger generation, but we may reach less. Every day that passes, however, is one less day to reach the second largest generation in America's history. And if previous patterns prove true, reaching the bridgers will become more difficult as they grow older.

We who are believers in Jesus Christ cannot be complacent. Our children who will soon be adults are receptive to the gospel today. But that moment of receptivity may soon pass. We who have hope in Jesus Christ must communicate that hope with urgency. The vast majority of the bridger generation does not have that hope. The consequences of the churches' response are eternal. The urgency is great. We cannot wait.

The Church: A Real and Present Hope for the Bridger Generation

Highlights

- Churches that reach bridgers will offer a community of unconditional love.
- Adult-to-bridger mentoring may be one of the most effective ways to reach this generation.
- Churches must be culturally sensitive to the bridger generation.
- Churches should teach the parents of bridgers how to reach their own children.
- The church must not abandon the doctrine of exclusivity.

> *What's the surest guarantee that an African-American urban youth will not fall to drugs or crime? Regular church attendance turns out to be a better predictor than family structure or income.*
>
> Richard Freeman
> Harvard University economist

My three bridger sons gathered around the kitchen table for one last "interview" about their generation. "Put up with the old man," I implored. I had a lot of research, a lot of interviews. Now I wanted to find out if my own kids were saying the same things I had heard from many of their bridger peers.

This time the question was about church, more specifically about their church. My three boys cannot wait to go to a Springdale Church service or function. The children's and youth programs are growing rapidly, and lives are being changed. OK, Sam, Art, and Jess: What is it about Springdale that is appealing to the bridger generation?

- "It's Tracy [the youth pastor]. His faith is real."
- "The people are cool. They let us have our own band and music."
- "Some of the reasons would have to include Pastor Butler's preaching. He's the best preacher I've ever heard . . . uh . . . of course, next to you, Dad."
- "The D-teams [disciple groups] are great. We really talk about some serious stuff in them."
- "All the kids are so involved, from regular Sunday ministries to mission trips to inner-city Boston to Indian reservations in South Dakota."
- "A bunch of adults give us a lot of time. They really seem to care about us."

My boys' comments were pretty close to the research we have gathered on America's second largest generation. What we have found is twofold. First, the bridgers have not given up on the church. Second, the church is a real and present hope for this generation. In my previous study of 576 of America's most evangelistic churches, we focused particularly on their ministry to youth and children.[1] We will look at the characteristics of their ministries shortly.

While Christians can understand the eternal importance of the church for the bridgers, it is interesting that the secular world is reaching that same conclusion, though for different reasons. "The link between religious participation and avoidance of drug abuse, alcoholism, crime, and other social pathologies is grist for new research,"[2] writes *U.S. News & World Report* reporters Joseph P. Shapiro and Andrea R. Wright. Brookings Institution political scientist John DiIulio comments, "It's remarkable how much good empirical evidence there is that religious belief can make a positive difference."[3] Shapiro and Wright cite a "survey by John Gartner of Loyola College of Maryland and David Larson of Duke University Medical Center [which] found over thirty studies that show a correlation between religious participation and avoidance of crime and substance abuse."[4]

Other statistics continue to grow which show the positive influence of church on all persons, particularly the bridgers:

- "The two most reliable predictors of teenage drug avoidance [are] optimism about the future and regular church attendance."[5]
- "The divorce rate for regular churchgoers is 18 percent; for those who attend services less than once a year, 24 percent."[6]
- "Frequent churchgoers are about 50 percent less likely to report psychological problems and 71 percent less likely to be alcoholics."[7]

Twelve Characteristics of Bridger-reaching Churches

The church is indeed a real and present hope for the bridgers. We already have evidence of churches that are reaching and impacting this generation. Though the characteristics are certainly not exhaustive, let us look at twelve traits of bridger-reaching churches.

Characteristic #1: Unconditional Love

The church can offer love and community that is like a family, though it cannot replace the nuclear family. Many of the bridgers have been rejected by their parents and peers. For them there is a great blessing in knowing that God accepts them in their sinfulness, that through Christ they will never face rejection from God.

But first these young people must see the love of Christ in the lives of the believers in the churches. This will challenge many believers. The bridgers are a new breed. They come from a different culture with a different vocabulary. They are not opposed to the culture of the church; they are simply ignorant of it. For too many years, too many churches have accepted only those who are like them. Bridger-reaching churches must not take that approach.

If a church can truly become a community of unconditional love, bridgers will flock to that church in unbelievable numbers. Such a community will not condone sinful and unacceptable behavior, but it will love bridgers with the same love that Christ loves us.

Will our churches be willing to change? This is the issue churches must face. Many churches will welcome gladly bridgers who come from families like theirs, but most bridgers are not from those kinds of families. The churches will have to decide what is more important, reaching a generation for Christ or guarding the status quo.

Characteristic #2: Adult-to-Bridger Mentoring

Less than three-fourths of the bridgers have two parents at home.[8] In many of the two-parent homes, only one will be a biological parent. More bridgers live with never-married mothers than has been the case in any previous generation.[9] And even in those homes where both biological parents are present, the likelihood is that both parents work. As we noted earlier, parents are spending less and less time with their children. One study found that working mothers spend an average of eleven minutes a day in meaningful time with their children on weekdays, and only thirty minutes a day on weekends. Working fathers did worse, averaging eight minutes a day with their kids on weekdays, and fourteen minutes a day on weekends.[10]

The children and youth of the bridger generation are starved for adult attention and interaction. And that need will not be met by one or a few adults standing before a large group of bridgers. They long for the one-on-one attention they are not receiving at home.

In two different studies of effective evangelistic churches across our nation, I noted a keen awareness of the need to reach young people before they reached adulthood. In many of the more effective churches, one-on-one mentoring and discipling was taking place between adults and youth. Indeed, in those churches that were reaching bridgers, this approach seemed to be among the most effective.

So why do not all churches begin an adult-to-youth mentoring program immediately? If this approach is so effective, why are only a few using it? The bridgers would welcome it, but the adult volunteers are too stressed out for time. Many of the Christian adults who are active in their churches are concerned about the limited time they spend with their own children. They cannot imagine finding time for kids who are not their own.

One church I visited found their solution in an often-overlooked group, senior adults. While most churches have ministries *to* senior adults, this church asked the older adults themselves to be ministers. Several began spending time one-on-one with a bridger. They studied Scripture together, had meals together, and even played together. The transformation in people from each generation has been miraculous.

Mentoring of bridgers by adults in the church will not be easy. But for the churches that decide these eternal lives are important, God will provide a way.

Characteristic #3: Intentional Evangelism

Perhaps one of my more interesting visits to a church took place when the pastor called me to discuss the low rate of conversion growth in a church. This large midwestern church was growing at a good rate. But, at the end of every year, the number of people reached for Christ was few, particularly for the size of the church.

The pastor and youth pastor were particularly concerned about how few youth the church evangelized each year. I began my consultation by asking questions about their youth ministry. The pastor and the youth pastor took me to their Wednesday-night "Solid Rock" program for teenagers. Nearly 150 young people were present. The music was good, the recreation was fun, and the speaker was obviously experienced in front of kids that particular age.

Again, as I toured the church, I saw excellent ministries, facilities, and activities for young persons. But something was missing, something that caused me to ask questions:

- "When do these kids hear the gospel?"
- "What intentional efforts are made to evangelize them?"
- "What are the specific plans each year to confront children and youth with the opportunity to make a decision for Christ?"

The silence that followed my questions gave me the unspoken answer. Rarely have I been in a church that had so many activities and opportunities for teenagers and children. But these kids were never confronted with their lostness, nor were they presented the gospel of Jesus Christ. Entertainment had won over evangelism.

My research team at The Southern Baptist Theological Seminary has studied almost one thousand churches that are reaching people for Christ. One consistent theme emanates from all of their ministries, activities, and programs: *intentionality in evangelism.* Churches can have a plethora of programs for bridgers, but without an explicit effort to reach them for Christ, the evangelistic results will be anemic. Evangelism is not a passive activity. Throughout Scripture, the emphases of evangelistic ministries are "go" and "tell."

Characteristic #4: High Expectations

As I mentioned briefly in the previous chapter, bridgers respond more readily when the church expects more of them. This factor surfaced repeatedly in our study of evangelistic churches. And when a church combined an intentionally evangelistic ministry to bridgers with high expectations, good evangelistic results were common.

A number of church leaders shared with us their weariness of low expectations that resulted in weak commitment. A Michigan pastor said, "I've been in churches all my life where church membership means no more than a group of people yelling 'Amen' after someone walks the aisle. That is nothing like the New Testament pattern of total commitment and discipleship. We have weak churches with apathetic members because we place no biblical expectations on them!"[11]

Many churches have discovered that low expectations and the search for the greatest level of seeker comfort have backfired. Instead of filling churches with new members who are committed Christians, they have been left with persons with a what-has-the-church-done-for-me-lately attitude.

Bridgers find themselves in schools that have "dumbed down" so that everyone can pass. Many bridgers are in homes of little or no discipline. They are hungry for a place that demonstrates unconditional love along with clear expectations. They are responding well to churches that demonstrate a belief that these kids are capable of meeting vigorous demands. They are just waiting for someone to tell them that they are smart enough to achieve something great. They will thrive in a church that teaches them that they can do anything in Christ's power. But they will avoid or leave quickly those churches that have no expectations for them. That low-expectation world is the one they are trying to leave.

Characteristic #5: Cultural Sensitivity

To be a high expectation church does not mean that a church is totally insensitive to the culture in which the bridgers live. To the contrary, a church still living in the 1950s is unlikely to reach the bridger generation.

What are particular areas of culture sensitivity of which the churches should be aware? As we reflect back upon some of the characteristics of the bridger generation, churches would do well to keep these traits in mind as they seek to reach the young people.

- They are a visual generation. Remember the words of one demographer: "They can take in and sort through visual information to a remarkable degree. They appreciate the subtleties of a media presentation—from a well-made special effect in a movie to an effective concept in a music video. They are comfortable with technology—really the first generation ever to be so. Don't underestimate the eventual impact of this characteristic."[12]

- They hate to be bored. They do not like delays or "down time." They have short attention spans.[13]
- They are very literal. Symbolism is often ineffective with bridgers.[14]
- They are stressed. "That blank look in the eye is neither laziness nor stupidity; today's young people are under tremendous stress and remoteness is a way to cope."[15]

But we must proceed with caution in our zeal to make our churches culturally-sensitive or seeker-sensitive. While bridgers appreciate churches that make cultural adjustments for them, they want to know that there is more to the church and to the faith it represents. Many churches have reached bridgers initially with user-friendly methodologies such as rock music and games. But these bridgers will also leave suddenly if they discover that beneath the cultural sensitivity was little substance. The kids will feel as if they have been manipulated or used.

Cultural sensitivity is a requisite to reach the bridger generation. But the church must demonstrate that their faith has substance beyond this initial attraction.

Characteristic #6: Biblical Preaching

In our study of 576 churches, we found an amazing correlation not only in preaching and evangelistic effectiveness, but also in preaching and reaching the bridgers.[16] Those pastors who gave a high priority to the preaching of God's Word led their churches to see lives changed in all age groups, and the bridgers were no exception.

The pastors we interviewed had a high view of Scripture. They believed not only in the truthfulness of the totality of God's Word; they also believed that it had power to change lives. Thus they preached with a sense of expectancy and urgency.[17]

Indeed, the bridgers in our focus groups across the country made numerous comments about their pastors. Many times we adults assume that the kids are not listening, but our research speaks to the contrary. "I really get something out of our pastor's preaching," one sixteen-year-old boy told us. "I mean he sticks with the Bible, but he helps me to understand what it means for me. And you can tell that he really believes everything in the Bible!"[18]

If we are to have any hope of reaching America's second largest generation for Christ, we must provide them teachings from God's own Word. Many of the mainline denominations have lost young people because the kids fail to see what is unique about the faith of their parents. C. Peter Wagner notes: "Studies of the denominations that have been losing members have shown that one factor across the board has been their inability to persuade their children to join their parents' churches."[19] Why? Because the children have not learned the essentials of their faith and how it makes a difference in this world . . . because preaching has been diluted, minimized, and proclaimed without authority.

Characteristic #7: Prayer Ministries

Another key factor in churches that reach bridgers is an emphasis on corporate prayer ministries. These churches not only emphasize prayer in each believer's life; they stress that the church must pray *together!* Two aspects of prayer ministries seem to be more closely related to reaching bridgers.

First, many of these churches are deliberately including bridgers in the prayer ministry. I visited seven churches in our evangelistic churches' research project that had more young people than adults involved in their prayer ministries. Bridgers indeed respond better when asked to *do* ministry.

Second, many of the churches we studied were praying specifically for the bridgers. One small church in Alabama has slightly less than thirty youth and children in attendance. For most of a month they dedicated one entire day for prayer for each of the youth. On those days when one of their own youth was not set aside for prayer, they dedicated the day to prayer for reaching youth in the community.

We should remember that some of the recent great awakenings of God in our nation have been led by bridgers. Chris Robeson, a student at Howard Payne University, was God's instrument who began a great revival at Coggin Avenue Baptist Church in Brownwood, Texas in February 1995.[20] And numerous students were used by God the following month as that same revival spread to places like Wheaton College and beyond.[21]

In our fascination with demographic trends, innovative methodologies, and culturally-sensitive ministries, we must not forget that only a sovereign God can send a revival to reach the bridgers. And if biblical patterns and revival history (see 2 Chron. 7:14) can be projected into the future, prayer will be used of God to precipitate these revivals.

Characteristic #8: Parental Training

The proportion of the bridger generation in the church today is less than in previous generations. We can surmise that many of the members in our churches have bridger children who are not involved in the church.

We have the opportunity to teach the adults in our churches to have a positive influence on their bridger children. As a consequence, many bridgers may choose to come to church; others who are attending may choose to stay.

What can we adults learn that can make a difference in the lives of our bridger children? When 100,000 children between the ages of eight and fourteen were asked what they wanted most in their parents, they named ten top items:

1. Parents who do not argue in front of them.
2. Parents who treat each member of the family the same.
3. Parents who are honest.
4. Parents who welcome their friends to the home.
5. Parents who are tolerant of others.
6. Parents who build a team spirit with their children.
7. Parents who answer their questions.
8. Parents who are consistent.
9. Parents who concentrate on their good points instead of their weaknesses.
10. Parents who give punishment when needed, but not in front of others, especially their friends.[22]

In his exhaustive study of today's youth culture, Walt Mueller cited several "gifts" we must provide our children in order to reach them for Christ.[23] First, we must give them unconditional love. This kind of love, says Mueller, "looks past the other person's faults, bad habits, imperfections, and unwillingness to love them back and continues to love. It is a commitment to love the unlovable, even when they don't deserve it."[24]

Second, we must give them our time. Fred Green is a juvenile probation officer who has interviewed hundreds of teens headed toward juvenile detention centers. He said he could summarize in one sentence the sentiments of the kids toward their parents: "Do not get hung up on a job that keeps you away from home."[25]

Related to the giving of time is the giving of attention. Mueller says without hesitation: "Parents, drop the paper, let the housework go, leave the briefcase at the office, and pay attention to your kids."[26]

Further, give them boundaries and consistent discipline. Fred Green gives further insight into what juvenile offenders say they wish their parents would do: "Shake me up. Punish me when I first go wrong. Tell me why. Convince me that more severe measures will come if I transgress again in the same manner. Call my bluff. Stand firm on what is right, even when your kid threatens to run away or become a delinquent or drop out of school. Stay in there with him and the bluffing will cease in 98 percent of the cases."[27]

Mueller also urges parents to be willing to admit their mistakes. I am not nearly as consistent as I should be, but some of the most precious moments I have experienced with each of my sons have been when I have told them I was wrong. Just a few weeks before I wrote these words, I got into a round of verbal warfare with one of my sons. I said several things I should not have said. Swallowing my parental pride an hour later, I entered his room to ask for forgiveness. His whole demeanor changed and he jokingly responded, "Oh Dad, I'll think about it and let you know in the next couple of weeks!"

Finally, says Mueller, we are to give our children a spiritual heritage. We must not only pray for them; we must also pray with them.

Such are some of the lessons the church can teach the parents. In 1980, shortly after the birth of my first son, Sam, I saw the "Focus on the Family" film series with James Dobson at Golden Springs Baptist Church in Anniston, Alabama. I thank God that the church invested a few hundred dollars to teach me how to be a parent. The film and its teachings changed my life. And I have to believe it ultimately impacted the lives of all three of my bridger sons.

Characteristic #9: Godly Youth Leadership

Among the key leadership positions in churches today should be those who lead our children and our youth. We should commit our resources of time and money for those leaders to be able to reach the bridger generation. One researcher is rather blunt about churches' failure to support youth leaders with adequate funding: "Churches spend the vast majority of their evangelistic dollars (more than 70 percent of it, by some of our preliminary research) trying to penetrate the adult market. After decades and decades of such toil, we can confidently announce the results: such efforts bear little fruit. On the other hand, the amount of money and effort we pour into reaching kids with the gospel pays off rather handsomely. The fact demands that we ask why we don't concentrate evangelistic efforts on youth."[28]

The churches that reach the bridgers in the twenty-first century will emphasize that some of the highest positions of leadership, whether paid or volunteer, will be positions of youth and children's leadership. The churches will seek the most godly and dedicated persons to lead these ministries. And the churches will support them enthusiastically with money, time, and prayers.

Characteristic #10: Effective Bible Study

Churches are losing young people because these young people have not learned the essentials and distinctives of their faith. Like their adult predecessors, the bridgers are woefully ignorant of the Bible. How can we expect to impact the lives of the bridger generation unless they understand the book which is our guide and direct word from God?

I have been pleading with churches for years to make certain they have ongoing opportunities for Bible study for all age groups. In my book *Giant Awakenings*, I particularly urged churches to look at their Sunday Schools to see if they are truly providing a method of teaching, with conviction and depth, the whole counsel of biblical truths to all ages.[29]

Dean R. Hoge, Benton Johnson, and Donald Luidens, three sociologists of mainline religion, came to this honest and compelling conclusion about mainline churches: "Our findings show that belief is the single best predictor of church participation, but it is orthodox Christian belief, and not the trends of lay liberalism, that impels people to be involved in the church."[30]

Further, the sociologists stress that these beliefs *must* be communicated to the next generations: "Unless the *youth* are firmly socialized into its tenets and standards, the strength of the religious community will eventually ebb away."[31] Sunday School has been among the key methodologies of the past two centuries to train adults *and* youth in the depths of the Bible. C. Peter Wagner agrees: "Some may say, 'But Sunday School is not part of our tradition.' This may be true, but if it is not, some functional substitute must be found."[32]

Characteristic #11: Exclusivity

Bridger-reaching churches of the twenty-first century will be bold and uncompromising in their stand that Christ is the only way of salvation. Many bridgers will resist that rigidity, calling it narrow-minded and prejudiced. But no bridger will be truly reached for Christ unless he or she comes through the Savior, believing Him to be the only way of salvation. Watch for this issue to be one of the most-debated theological issues of the early twenty-first century.

Characteristic #12: **Involved Youth**

Finally, a notable characteristic of bridger-reaching churches will be the involvement of their youth in ministry. These churches will not be satisfied to fill the pews with bridgers; they will make every effort to involve each young person in ministry.

Several years ago, when I was a pastor in Louisville, Kentucky, I made a few comments regarding the "youth week" emphasis in which our church was involved. In the course of my comments, I spoke of the youth being "the future of our church and nation." After the service, one of our volunteer youth leaders mildly chastised me. She said, "Pastor, these kids are not just our future; they are our present as well."

I appreciated the rebuke. She reminded me that most churches see the youth as a group who will *one day* be contributors to the church and to society. But a bridger-reaching church realizes that this generation has a lot to offer today. And the likelihood of their coming to our churches and staying in them is enhanced when we stress their involvement. Bridgers are not waiting to make a difference one day in the future. They are ready to accept the challenge today.

A Postscript

I am both fearful and trusting. I am fearful because the second largest generation in America is slipping away. According to our best estimates and statistical measures, we are reaching fewer for Christ from the bridger generation than from any previous generation. But I am trustful as well. I believe in a God who is not done with our nation and her youth. I believe that the churches in America will rise to the challenge to touch their lives for Christ.

I want to thank you for taking this journey with me. As I wrote this book, my emotions moved from hope to worry to despair to fear and back to hope again. It has truly been an emotional roller coaster. There *is* much to fear as we look at the bridger generation. But we serve a God who is bigger than the biggest obstacle we will ever face. So I end this book with hope.

It is my prayer that, in the midst of the data, trends, and analyses, you have been challenged. I pray that you have seen the urgency of the hour to reach this generation *now*, not later. And I pray that your church will be willing to make those changes necessary to reach the bridgers.

Though I have written several books, this is my first generational book. Though I have enjoyed reading about the boomers and busters, I have not had an inclination to write about them.

Then came my awareness of the bridger generation, the second largest generation in America's history, the generation that includes my three sons.

You see, I have tried to be a good father to Sam, Art, and Jess. I have tried to give them time. And I do give them unconditional love. I pray with them regularly. I wept as each of the boys made his commitment to Jesus Christ.

But I still worry. I know that my boys see my faults clearly. I know that I have traveled some days when I should have stayed at home. I know that I have lost my temper more times than I care to admit. And I know that I have been less than the perfect husband to their mother.

How will my three boys fare as adults in this tough world? Will they remember my many faults or my few strengths? Will God be first in all they do? Did I fail or pass as a father?

Many years ago, when all three of my sons were preschool age, I came across a prayer written by General Douglas MacArthur. I adapted it a bit, made a copy of it, and have kept it in my Bible for nearly twelve years. May I share it with you?

A Prayer
From an Imperfect Father
For His Three Priceless Sons

By Thom S. Rainer

Make me the father, O Lord
Who will show my sons the strength to face weakness;
The courage to face fear;
The grace to accept honest defeat;
And the humility and gentleness to accept victory.

Make me the father
Who will show my sons not a path of ease and comfort,
But the ability to accept the challenge of stress and difficulty.
Use me, I pray, to be the example of one who can stand up in the storm,
And there learn compassion for those who fail.

Make me the father
Who will teach his sons the value of a clear heart and a high goal;
To master themselves before they seek to master others;
To learn to laugh, yet never forget how to cry;
To reach into the future without forgetting the past.

Make me the father, O Lord,
Who will show my sons enough of a sense of humor,
So they will always be serious,
But never take themselves too seriously.
Give them humility,
So they will always remember the simplicity of true greatness,
The open mind of true wisdom,
And the meekness of true strength.

And after all these things are theirs,
Add for me, I pray,
The wisdom to show them the dubious value
Of titles, positions, money, and material gain,
And the eternal value
Of prayer, the Holy Bible, a Christian home,
And a saving relationship with Your Son Jesus Christ.

Then I, their father,
Will dare to whisper,
"I have not lived in vain."

May we go forth to win a generation for Christ. But may we go forth with the assurance that God will be with us wherever we go. And with that promise we can now claim the bridger generation for Jesus Christ.

NOTES

Introduction

1. Susan Mitchell, *The Official Guide to Generations* (Ithaca, N.Y.: New Strategist Publications, 1995), xxii.
2. Ibid., 1.
3. Jeff Giles, "Generalizations X," *Newsweek*, 6 June 1994, 63.
4. Ibid.
5. Susan Mitchell, "The Next Baby Boom," *American Demographics*, xvii, no. 10, (October 1995), 25.
6. Cited in Mitchell, "Next Baby Boom," 25.
7. Mitchell, "Next Baby Boom," 26. The bridgers cited in this statistic were ages twelve to seventeen in 1995.
8. Ibid.
9. Ibid.
10. Ibid., 26–27.
11. Ibid., 27.
12. Ibid.
13. Cited in Mitchell, "Next Baby Boom," 25.
14. See, for example, John Avant, Malcom McDow, and Alvin Reid, eds., *Revival!* (Nashville: Broadman and Holman, 1996).
15. See Thom S. Rainer, *Effective Evangelistic Churches* (Nashville: Broadman and Holman, 1996) for the results of an empirical study on 576 evangelistic churches in America. The renewed emphasis on expository preaching and Sunday School is discussed extensively in this book.
16. Mitchell, "Next Baby Boom," 31.

Chapter 1

1. The survey was entitled "Teenage Update 1995." It involved telephone interviews with a random sample of 723 bridgers (a term Barna does not use) between the ages of thirteen and eighteen. The interviews were conducted in December 1994 and January 1995. This information is in George Barna, *Generation Next* (Ventura, Calif.: Regal, 1995), 38.
2. Susan Mitchell, "The Next Baby Boom," *American Demographics*, (October 1995), 24. Mitchell cites a survey by the American Freshman Higher Education Research Institute, University of California-Los Angeles.
3. Robert Friendman, "Introduction," *Life* (The Baby Boom Turns 50 Special Issue), 15 July 1996, 12.
4. Barna, *Generation Next*, 26.
5. Ibid.
6. Ibid, 43.

7. "The Case for Tough Standards," *U.S. News & World Report*, 1 April 1996, 52.
8. Ibid.
9. Ibid., 52–57.
10. Chip Alford, "A Resource for Time-savvy Teens," *Facts and Trends*, April 1996, 4.
11. Barna, *Generation Next*, 42.
12. Eric Miller with Mary Porter, *In the Shadow of the Baby Boom* (Brooklyn, NY: EPM Communications, 1994), 5.
13. Ibid., 36.
14. From a focus group interview conducted by the author, March 1996.
15. Miller, *In the Shadow*, 6.
16. Ibid., 4.
17. Ibid., 7.
18. Mitchell, "The Next Baby Boom" 24.
19. Ibid.
20. Miller, *In the Shadow*, 5.
21. Ibid., 38.
22. Teenage Research Unlimited, Wave 21/Spring 1993, cited in Miller, *In the Shadow*, 38.
23. Miller, *In the Shadow*, 38.
24. Ibid.
25. Ibid., 7.
26. Ibid., 11.
27. Ibid., 19.
28. Ibid., 4.
29. From a focus group interview conducted by the author, October 1995.
30. Ibid.
31. Barna, *Generation Next*, 76.
32. Focus group interview, March 1996.
33. Barna, *Generation* Next, 79.
34. Ibid., 74, emphasis added.
35. From a focus group interview conducted by the author, October 1995. Our research on the boomer phenomenon is discussed in my book *Giant Awakenings* (Nashville: Broadman and Holman, 1995), particularly pages 51–56.
36. Dean R. Hoge, Benton Johnson, and Donald D. Luidens, *Vanishing Boundaries: The Religion of Mainline Protestant Baby Boomers* (Louisville: Westminster/John Knox, 1994), 200.
37. See Thom S. Rainer, *Effective Evangelistic Churches* (Nashville: Broadman and Holman, 1996).
38. See Barna, *Generation Next*, 79–80.

Chapter 2

1. Richard Louv, *Childhood's Future* (New York: Anchor Books, 1990), 6.
2. Cited in Louv, 6.
3. Quoted in Louv, 46.
4. Susan Mitchell, "The Next Baby Boom," *American Demographics* (October 1995), 23–24.
5. Ibid., 24.
6. Ibid., 31.

7. Ibid., 30.

8. From Census Bureau statistics

9. Mitchell, "The Next Baby Boom," 30.

10. Eric Miller, with Mary Porter, *In the Shadow of the Baby Boom* (Brooklyn, N.Y.: EPM Communications, 1994), 39.

11. Ibid.

12. Ibid.

13. Ibid., 39.

14. Ibid.

15. George Barna, *Generation Next* (Ventura, Calif.: Regal, 1995), 32.

16. Cited in Walt Mueller, *Understanding Today's Youth Culture* (Wheaton, Ill: Tyndale, 1994), 213.

17. Ibid.

18. Ibid.

19. Ibid.

20. Ted Gest, with Victoria Pope, "Crime Time Bomb," *U.S. News & World Report*, (25 March 1996), 36.

21. Ibid., 30.

22. Mitchell, "The Next Baby Boom," 27.

23. Ibid.

24. Ibid.

25. Ibid.

26. Cited in Mitchell, 27.

27. Edward Cornish, "The Cyber Future," *The Futurist*, January/ February 1996, special insert section, 1–15.

28. Ibid., 2.

29. Ibid.

30. Thom S. Rainer, *Effective Evangelistic Churches* (Nashville: Broadman & Holman, 1996).

31. Dean R. Hoge, Benton Johnson, and Donald Luidens, *Vanishing Boundaries: The Religion of Mainline Protestant Baby Boomers* (Louisville: Westminster/John Knox, 1994), 178.

32. Ibid., 199.

33. Based on a research project in the Billy Graham School of Missions, Evangelism, and Church Growth, The Southern Baptist Theological Seminary, Louisville, Kentucky, in 1996.

34. Ibid.

Chapter 3

1. Jerrold K. Footlick, "What Happened to the Family?" *Newsweek* (special edition), winter/spring 1990, 15.

2. Eric Miller, with Mary Porter, *In the Shadow of the Baby Boom* (Brooklyn, N.Y.: EPM Communications, 1994), 5.

3. One research study concludes that up to 60 percent of the children born in the nineties will be a product of a single-parent home. See Frank F. Burstenburg Jr., and Andrew J. Cherlin, *Divided Families: What Happens to Children When Parents Part* (Cambridge, Mass.: Harvard University Press, 1991), 11.

4. Judith Wallerstein and Sandra Blackesless, *Second Chances: Men, Women and Children a Decade after Divorce* (New York: Tickner and Fields, 1989).

5. Walt Mueller, *Understanding Today's Youth Culture* (Wheaton, Ill.: Tyndale House, 1994), 41.

6. Ibid.

7. Miller, *In the Shadow*, 6–7.

8. Ibid., 7.

9. See Thom S. Rainer, *Eating the Elephant* (Nashville: Broadman and Holman, 1994), 24–25.

10. Mueller, *Understanding Today's Youth Culture*, 41.

11. Ibid., 53–54.

12. Cited in Mueller, 42.

13. U.S. Census Bureau, "Household Family Characteristics" March 1993.

14. "What Parents Don't Know," *Parents and Teenagers*, February/ March 1989, 2. Cited in Mueller, 47.

15. Susan Mitchell, "The Next Baby Boom," *American Demographics* (October 1995), 26.

16. Ibid., 26–27.

17. Cited in Mueller, 44.

18. Mueller, *Understanding Today's Youth Culture*, 44.

19. Cited in Mueller, 45.

20. Donald A. Atkinson and Charles L. Roesel, *Meeting Needs, Sharing Christ* (Nashville: LifeWay Press, 1995), 9.

21. Ibid., 26.

Chapter 4

1. "Crime Time Bomb," *U. S. News & World Report*, 25 March 1996, 29.

2. Ibid.

3. Ibid.

4. From a focus group interview conducted by the author, March, 1996.

5. Susan Mitchell, *The Official Guide to the Generations* (Ithaca, N.Y.: New Strategist, 1995), 342–43.

6. Ibid.

7. Eric Miller, with Mary Porter, *In the Shadow of the Baby Boom* (Brooklyn, N.Y.: EPM Communications, 1994), 45.

8. Ibid.

9. Ibid.

10. "Crime Time Bomb."

11. Walt Mueller, *Understanding Today's Youth Culture* (Wheaton, Ill.: Tyndale House, 1994), 279–84.

12. Ibid., 281.

13. Ibid.

14. Ibid., 282.

15. Ibid.

16. Ibid.

17. "Crime Time Bomb," 36.

18. Ibid., 30.

19. Focus group interview, March, 1996.

20. "Crime Time Bomb," 32.
21. Miller, *In the Shadow,* 45.
22. "Crime Time Bomb," 36.
23. Richard Louv, *Childhood's Future* (New York: Anchor Books, 1990), 165.
24. Miller, *In the Shadow,* 45.
25. Louv, *Childhood's Future,* 105.
26. Mueller, *Understanding Today's Youth Culture,* 10.
27. Ibid.
28. "A Pittsburgh Court Battles the Tide," *U. S. News & World Report,* 25 March 1996, 37.
29. Susan Mitchell, "The Next Baby Boom," *American Demographics* (October 1995), 25 26.
30. Ibid., 26.
31. "Crime Time Bomb," 36.
32. Ibid.
33. Mitchell, "The Next Baby Boom," 27.
34. Ibid.
35. Ibid.
36. Ibid., 30.
37. Ibid.
38. Ibid.
39. Ibid.
40. Ibid.
41. "Colorado Has a New Brand of Tough Love," *U.S. News & World Report,* 25 March 1996, 38.
42. Ibid.
43. Ibid.
44. Ibid.
45. Ibid.
46. "A Pittsburgh Court Battles the Tide," 37.
47. Ibid.
48. Ibid.
49. Ibid.
50. Mueller, *Understanding Today's Youth Culture,* 37–38.
51. See Thom S. Rainer, *Effective Evangelistic Churches* (Nashville: Broadman & Holman, 1996).
52. From the study published in *Effective Evangelistic Churches.*

Chapter 5

1. "The American Freshman," Higher Education Research Institute, University of California-Los Angeles (1992). These percentages actually apply to incoming freshmen rather than the entire bridger population.
2. Ibid.
3. Focus group discussion in Georgia, January 1996.
4. Census Bureau data.
5. Ibid.
6. Ibid.

7. "Kids Count DataBook," The Center for the Study of Social Policy, cited in Eric Miller with Mary Porter, *In the Shadow of the Baby Boom* (Brooklyn, NY: EPM Communications), 11.

8. Eric Miller with Mary Porter, *In the Shadow of the Baby Boom* (Brooklyn, N.Y.: EPM Communications), 12.

9. Walt Mueller, *Understanding Today's Youth Culture* (Wheaton, Ill.: Tyndale, 1994), 237.

10. Ibid., 238, emphasis in original.

11. "The American Freshman."

12. "The Family—Surviving Tough Times in the '90's," American Board of Family Practice, cited in Eric Miller, with Mary Porter, *In the Shadow of the Baby Boom* (Brooklyn, N.Y.: EPM Communications), 45.

13. Ibid.

14. "Teens Still Believe in the Dream," *The Numbers News*, June 1996, 5.

15. Ibid. The data for this article came from *YOUTHviews*, The George H. Gallup International Institute, n.d.

16. Carrie Goerne, "Marketers Try to Get More Creative in Reaching Teens," *Marketing News*, 5 August 1991, 2.

17. William Ecenbarger, "A Nation of Thieves," *Philadelphia Inquirer Magazine*, 29 November 1987, 22, cited in Mueller, 239.

18. Cited in Mueller, 238.

19. Cited in Mueller, 240.

20. Mueller, *Understanding Today's Youth Culture*, 240.

21. Steve Waldman and Karen Springen, "Too Old, Too Fast?" *Newsweek*, 16 November 1992, 87.

22. Ibid., 81.

23. Ibid.

24. Ibid.

25. Cited in Mueller, 241.

26. Ibid.

27. Ibid.

28. Ron Harris, "For Too Many Youths, Clothing an Obsession," *Philadelphia Inquirer*, 23 November 1989, I–7, cited in Mueller, 243.

29. Rick Telander, "Your Sneakers or Your Life," *Sports Illustrated*, 14 May 1990, 36–49, cited in Mueller, 244.

30. Rodney Clapp, "Why the Devil Takes Visa," *Christianity Today*, 7 October 1996, 20.

31. Ibid., 20–21.

32. Ibid.

33. John Naisbitt, *John Naisbitt's Trend Letter*, 26 October 1995, 1.

34. Miller, *In the Shadow*, 19.

35. Ibid.

36. Mueller, *Understanding Today's Youth Culture*, 249.

37. C. S. Lewis, *Mere Christianity* (New York: Macmillan, 1952), 120.

Chapter 6

1. The television data relate to teens age 12–17; source: 1992–93 Nielsen Report on Television. Other data are for teenagers; source: Teenage Research Unlimited,

Wave 21/Spring 1993. Both sets of data came from Eric Miller, with Mary Porter, *In the Shadow of the Baby Boom* (Brooklyn, N.Y.: EPM, 1994), 38.

2. Eric Miller, with Mary Porter, *In the Shadow of the Baby Boom* (Brooklyn , N.Y.: EPM, 1994), 38.

3. George Comstock, *Television in America* (Beverly Hills: Sage, 1980), ix.

4. Nancy Ten Kate, "TV Dynasty," *American Demographics* (January 1991), 16.

5. Jane Delano Brown et al., "The Influence of New Media and Family Structure on Young Adolescents' Television and Radio Use," *Communication Research*, 17, no. 1 (February 1990): 72, cited in Walt Mueller, *Understanding Today's Youth Culture* (Wheaton, Ill.: Tyndale, 1994), 125.

6. Miller, *In the Shadow*, 39.

7. Ibid.

8. Ibid., 40. Miller states that the older bridgers, teenagers, account for approximately 30 percent of sales. The younger bridgers, age twelve and under, account for the remaining 20 percent.

9. Cited in Miller, 40.

10. *Implications* 5, Fall 1992, 18, cited in Mueller, 139.

11. Josh McDowell, *Teen Sex Survey in the Evangelical Church: Executive Summary Report 1987*, 15, cited in Mueller, 139.

12. Source: Movie Morality Ministries, cited in Mueller, 140.

13. Miller, *In the Shadow*, 39.

14. Ibid.

15. Ibid.

16. Mueller, *Understanding Today's Youth Culture*, 127.

17. Ibid., 128.

18. Ibid., 129.

19. From a focus study group in Kentucky, 1996.

20. Cited in Mueller, 130.

21. Mueller, *Understanding Today's Youth Culture*, 131.

22. Ibid.

23. Barry S. Sapolsky and Joseph O. Tabarlet, "Sex in Primetime Television: 1979 Versus 1989," *Journal of Broadcasting and Electronic Media*, 125, no. 4 (Fall 1991): 514, cited in Mueller, 132.

24. Mueller, *Understanding Today's Youth Culture*, 136.

25. Ibid., 78.

26. Quentin J. Schultze et al., *Dancing in the Dark* (Grand Rapids: Eerdmans, 1991), 192.

27. Ibid.

28. George Barna, *Generation Next* (Ventura, Calif.: Regal, 1995), 53.

29. Ibid., 54.

30. Schultze, *Dancing in the Dark*, 12–13.

31. See Mueller, *Understanding Today's Youth Culture*, 81–100, for a good and more thorough overview of these values.

32. Mueller, *Understanding Today's Youth Culture*, 86.

33. Ibid.

34. Ibid., 88.

35. Ibid., 90.

36. Ibid., 97.

37. Ibid.

38. Cited in Mueller, 99.

39. "A New Look at the Internet," *Forecast* 16, no. 10 (October 1996): 1.

40. Ibid.

41. Rick Warren, *The Purpose Driven Church* (Grand Rapids: Zondervan, 1995), 208–209.

42. Ibid., 216.

43. Ibid., 236.

Chapter 7

1. George Barna, *Generation Next* (Ventura, Calif.: Regal, 1995), 39.

2. National Center for Health Statistics, *Statistical Abstract of the United States—1994*, U.S. Bureau of the Census, 1994.

3. Ibid.

4. Eric Miller, with Mary Porter, *In the Shadow of the Baby Boom* (Brooklyn: EPM Communications, 1994), 45. Most of the statistics cited by Miller come from "The Family—Surviving Tough Times in the 90s," American Board of Family Practice.

5. Barna, *Generation Next*, 25.

6. Ibid.

7. From a focus group in Florida, 1995.

8. Ibid.

9. Ibid.

10. Judith Wallerstein and Sandra Blakeslee, *Second Chances: Men, Women and Children a Decade after Divorce* (New York: Tickner & Fields, 1989).

11. Walt Mueller, *Understanding Today's Youth Culture* (Wheaton, Ill. Tyndale, 1994), 41.

12. Ibid.

13. Miller, *In the Shadow*, 45.

14. Ibid.

15. Ibid.

16. Barna, *Generation Next*, 27.

17. Susan Mitchell, "The Next Baby Boom," *American Demographics* (October 1995), 31.

18. Ibid.

19. Mitchell, "The Next Baby Boom," 24. Her source is The American Freshman Higher Education Research Institute, University of California-Los Angeles.

20. Ibid.

21. Barna, *Generation Next*, 29.

22. Miller, *In the Shadow*, 45.

23. Cited in Mueller, 34–35.

24. Miller, *In the Shadow*, 45.

25. Mueller, *Understanding Today's Youth Culture*, 34–35.

26. Ibid., 35.

27. Miller, *In the Shadow*, 45.

28. Ibid.

29. From a focus group, Tennessee, 1996.

30. Eugene Roehlkepartain, ed., "How Much Time with Friends," in *Youth Ministry Resource Book* (Loveland, Colo.: Group Books, 1988), 37ff. Cited in Mueller, 185.

31. Mueller, *Understanding Today's Youth Culture,* 185.
32. Cited in Mueller, 185.
33. Mueller, *Understanding Today's Youth Culture,* 190–96.
34. Cited in Miller, 45.
35. Barna, *Generation Next,* 32.
36. Chip Alford, "A Resource for Time-Savvy Teens," *Facts and Trends,* April 1996, 4.
37. From a focus group in Tennessee, 1996.
38. "The Family: Surviving Tough Times in the 90s," American Board of Family Practice. Cited in Miller, 45.
39. From a focus group in Tennessee, 1996.
40. Mueller, *Understanding Today's Youth Culture,* 213.
41. Ibid.
42. Ibid., 214.
43. Ibid.
44. Ibid.
45. Ibid.
46. Ibid.
47. Ibid.
48. Ibid.
49. Ibid.
50. Ibid.
51. "The Family: Surviving Tough Times in the 90s," American Board of Family Practice. Cited in Miller, 45.
52. Mueller, *Understanding Today's Youth Culture,* 216.
53. From a focus group in Florida, 1995.
54. American Board of Family Practice. Cited in Miller, 8.
55. "What Makes Teens Tick," Kaplao Education Center. Cited in Miller, 9.
56. From a focus group in Florida, 1995.
57. From a focus group in Georgia, 1995.

Chapter 8

1. One such recommendation would be John Avant, Malcom McDow, and Alvin Reid. *Revival!* (Nashville: Broadman & Holman, 1995).
2. Bill Moyers, "America's Religious Mosaic," *USA Weekend,* 11–13 October 1996, 4.
3. Ibid.
4. Ibid.
5. Joseph P. Shapiro, with Andrea R. Wright, "Can Churches Save America?" *U.S. News & World Report,* 9 September 1996, 49.
6. Moyers, "America's Religious Mosaic," 4.
7. Ibid.
8. Susan Mitchell, "The Next Baby Boom," *American Demographics* (October 1995), 24–25.
9. Ibid.
10. From a Census Bureau report, cited in Mitchell, 25.
11. Mitchell, "The Next Baby Boom," 25.
12. Ibid.
13. Ibid.
14. Ibid.

15. Ibid., 25–26.
16. These projections are based on hard data from the Census Bureau with the exception of homosexual parents. The latter is based upon recent surveys indicating greater acceptance of homosexual marriages, legislative efforts to recognize such marriages, and corporate benefits provided to homosexual parents.
17. Mitchell, "The Next Baby Boom," 26.
18. Eric Miller, with Mary Porter, *In the Shadow of the Baby Boom* (Brooklyn, N.Y.: EPM Communications, 1994), 8.
19. Ibid., 45.
20. Ibid.
21. Ibid., 36.
22. Ibid.
23. Ibid.
24. Ibid., 37.
25. *John Naisbitt's Trend Letter*, Vol. 15, No. 14, 15, February 1996, 1.
26. Edward Cornish, "'The Cyber Future' 92 Ways Our Lives Will Change by the Year 2025," *The Futurist*, January/February 1996, special insert, 2.
27. Ibid.
28. Ibid.
29. Ibid., 4.
30. Ibid.
31. Ibid., 7.
32. Ibid., 10.
33. Ibid., 12.
34. Ibid.
35. Ibid.
36. Ibid., 15.
37. Mitchell, "The Next Baby Boom,"30.
38. Ibid.
39. Ibid.
40. *John Naisbitt's Trend Letter*, 15 February 1996, 3.
41. Ibid.
42. Ibid., 4.
43. Ibid.
44. Ibid.
45. Ibid.
46. *Roper's The Public Pulse*, Vol. 10, No. 1, January 1995, 3.
47. *John Naisbitt's Trend Letter*, Vol. 15, No. 1, 4 January 1996, 1–2.
48. Cornish, 4.
49. Ibid.
50. *Roper's The Public Pulse*, 5.
51. Ibid.
52. Cornish, 4.
53. Ibid.
54. Ibid., 4–5.
55. William S. Rukeyser, "Let's Do the Hobble: The Generation That Won't Go Away." *Next*. Vol. 1, No. 2, August 1995, 14.
56. *John Naisbitt's Trend Letter*, Vol. 14, No. 21, 26 October 1995, 1.
57. Mitchell, 31.

Chapter 9

1. From a focus group in Georgia, 1995.
2. Bill Moyers, "America's Religious Mosaic," *USA Weekend*, 11–13 October 1996, 5.
3. Ibid.
4. Pam Janis, "God Pops Up in Culture," *USA Weekend*, 11–13 October 1996, 6.
5. Ibid.
6. Moyers, 4.
7. Ibid.
8. Ibid.
9. Ibid.
10. Ibid.
11. From *Britannica Book of the Year, 1995*, cited in Moyers, 5.
12. George Barna, *Generation Next* (Ventura, Calif.: Regal, 1995), 74.
13. Ibid, 75.
14. Ibid, 79.
15. Ibid.
16. Ibid.
17. Ibid., 81.
18. Ibid.
19. Ibid., 75.
20. Ibid., 75–81.
21. Ronald H. Nash, *Is Jesus the Only Savior?* (Grand Rapids: Zondervan, 1994), 21–22.
22. See for example John Hick, *God Has Many Names* (London: Macmillan, 1980).
23. Wilfred Cantrell Smith, "An Attempt at Summation," in *Christ's Lordship and Religious Pluralism*, ed. G. H. Anderson and T. F. Stransky (Mary Knoll, N.Y.: Orbis, 1981), 202.
24. Joseph Runzo, "God, Commitment and Other Faiths: Pluralism vs. Relativism," *Faith and Philosophy* 5 (1988): 357.
25. Nash, 95.
26. John Hick, *Problems of Religious Pluralism* (New York: St. Martin's Press, 1985), 34.
27. Nash, 22.
28. Ibid.
29. John Hick, "Jesus and the World Religions," in *The Myth of God Incarnate*, ed. John Hick (London: SCM, 1977), 180.
30. Nash, 103.
31. John Sanders, *No Other Name* (Grand Rapids: Eerdmans, 1992), 131.
32. Clark H. Pinnock, "The Finality of Jesus Christ in a World of Religions," in *Christian Faith and Practice in the Modern World*, ed. Mark A. Noll and David F. Wells (Grand Rapids: Eerdmans, 1988), 153.
33. Ibid.
34. Clark H. Pinnock, *A Wideness in God's Mercy* (Grand Rapids: Zondervan, 1992), 96.
35. Ibid., 97.
36. Ibid., 112.
37. Ibid.

38. Nash, 107.
39. Ibid., 11.
40. Ibid., 12.
41. See chapter 10, where I discuss this research and its implications.
42. John Hick, *Disputed Questions in Theology and Philosophy* (New Haven: Yale University, 1993), viii.
43. Nash, 95.
44. Moyers, 5.
45. Ibid.
46. Barna, 32.
47. Ibid.
48. Ibid.
49. Ibid.
50. Ibid., 98–103.
51. Ibid., 106.
52. Ibid.

Chapter 10

1. This survey was conducted by me in three states over a seven-month period in 1995 and 1996.
2. Ibid.
3. This survey was conducted by me in seventeen states over a fifteen-month period in 1995 and 1996.
4. George Barna, *Generation Next* (Ventura, Calif.: Regal, 1995), 77.
5. Ibid.
6. Ibid.
7. C. Peter Wagner, *Church Growth and the Whole Gospel: A Biblical Mandate* (San Francisco: Harper & Row, 1981), 77.
8. Ibid.
9. Ibid., 77–78.
10. C. Peter Wagner, *Strategies for Church Growth* (Ventura, Calif.: Regal, 1987), 67.
11. Ibid.
12. Barna, 78.
13. Ibid., 79.
14. See Thom S. Rainer, *Effective Evangelistic Churches* (Nashville: Broadman & Holman, 1996), 20–22.
15. Ibid., 23.
16. Ibid., 20.
17. Ibid., 21.
18. Barna, 74, 878–88.
19. I am referring to the material in my book *Effective Evangelistic Churches* cited earlier.
20. "The Family—Surviving Tough Times in the Nineties," American Board of Family Practice, cited in Eric Miller with Mary Porter, *In the Shadow of the Baby Boom* (Brooklyn, N.Y.: EPM Communications, 1994), 45.
21. From a focus group in Georgia, 1995.
22. Rainer, *Effective Evangelistic Churches,* 20–22.

Chapter 11

1. See Thom S. Rainer, *Effective Evangelistic Churches* (Nashville: Broadman & Holman, 1996).

2. Joseph P. Shapiro and Andrea R. Wright, "Can Churches Save America?" *U.S. News & World Report*, 9 September 1996, 50.

3. Ibid.

4. Ibid.

5. Ibid.

6. Ibid.

7. Ibid.

8. Susan Mitchell, "The Next Baby Boom," *American Demographics* (October 1995), 24.

9. Ibid.

10. David Elkind, *Miseducation* (New York: Knopf, 1987), 24. Cited in Walt Mueller, *Understanding Today's Youth* (Wheaton: Tyndale House, 1994), 41.

11. Rainer, 174.

12. Eric Miller, with Mary Porter, *In the Shadow of the Baby Boom* (Brooklyn, N.Y.: EPM Communications, 1994), 5.

13. Ibid., 3.

14. Ibid., 4.

15. Ibid.

16. See Rainer, especially chapter 3.

17. Ibid., 51.

18. From a focus group in Florida, 1995.

19. C. Peter Wagner, *The Healthy Church* (Ventura, Calif.: Regal, 1996), 146.

20. See John Avant, Malcom McDow, and Alvin Reid, eds. in *Revival!* (Nashville: Broadman & Holman, 1996), especially chapter 3.

21. See Timothy Beougher and Lyle Dosett, eds., *Accounts of a Campus Revival* (Wheaton: Harold Shaw, 1995).

22. "Parental Behavior," *Coral Ridge Encounter*, April 1990, 41. Cited in Mueller, 340.

23. Mueller, *Understanding Today's Youth Culture*, 340–44.

24. Ibid., 340.

25. Ibid., 341.

26. Ibid., 342

27. Ibid., 343.

28. George Barna, *Generation Next* (Ventura, Calif.: Regal, 1995), 77.

29. See Thom S. Rainer, *Giant Awakenings* (Nashville: Broadman & Holman, 1995), especially chapter 3.

30. Dean R. Hoge, Benton Johnson, and Donald A. Luidens, *Vanishing Boundaries: The Religion of Mainline Protestant Baby Boomers* (Louisville, Ky.: Westminster/John Knox, 1994), 185.

31. Ibid., 183

32. Wagner, 147.

INDEX

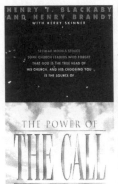

The Power Of The Call

Henry T. Blackaby & Henry Brandt

This encouraging look at leadership strengthens and inspires weary pastors and church leaders by reminding them of God's powerful call. Redemptive conversations reveal God's goodness and sovereignty. This book examines the heart of a true church leader, acknowledging sinful tendencies while offering suggestions on how ministers and members of their congregations can strengthen any pastor's ministry. An excellent revitalizing tool for all pastors and leaders.   0-8054-6297-X

Out Of Their Faces & Into Their Shoes

How To Understand Spiritually Lost People and Give Them Directions To God

John Kramp

This entertaining yet richly spiritual book shows that effective witnessing depends not on gospel show-downs, but on using "lostology" to understand another's point of view.

0-8054-6350-X

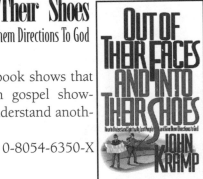

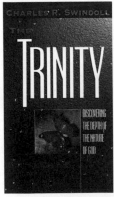

The "Growing Deep In The Christian Life" series

Charles R. Swindoll

This five volume study series by one of America's most popular preachers helps Christians increase their discernment and understanding in five vital areas of the Christian faith.

The Trinity	0-8054-0162-8
The Bible	0-8054-0160-1
Eternity	0-8054-0157-1
The Family Of God	0-8054-0161-X
Salvation	0-8054-0158-X

AVAILABLE AT FINE CHRISTIAN BOOKSTORES EVERYWHERE

...More Insights For *Your Ministry*

The Insights For Ministry Collection

Creating Community • *Deeper Fellowship Through Small Group Ministry*
Dr. Glen S. Martin & Dr. Gary L. McIntosh

In an age of change and uncertainty, small group fellowships provide the support and care that other source can offer. *Creating Community* contains valuable advice for starting and nurturing a small group ministry. Written by two leading experts on church growth, this book gives congregations both the will and the skill to become effective witnesses in this dynamic form of ministry.

0-8054-6100-0

Effective Evangelistic Churches • *Successful Churches Reveal What Works & What Doesn't*
Thom S. Rainer

Part research project, part detective story, this book presents results from the most comprehensive study of successful churches in history. These 586 churches across America all excel in winning new souls for Christ, and have a remarkable range of things in common. Some stereotypes are shattered, some results are astonishing, and everything is written in readable, non-technical style.

0-8054-5402-0

Revitalizing The Sunday Morning Dinosaur • *A Sunday School Growth Strategy For The 21st Century*
Ken Hemphill

Some church leaders consider Sunday School to be a tired old dinosaur. But according to church growth expert Ken Hemphill, Sunday School is not only still relevant, it's the key to integrated church growth for the next century. In *Revitalizing the Sunday Morning Dinosaur,* Dr. Hemphill describes how a well-crafted Sunday School program can propel any church to new levels of growth and outreach.

0-8054-6174-4

Putting An End To Worship Wars • *Elmer Towns*

In searching for the most meaningful form of worship, congregations sometimes find differences that tear them apart. Church leaders fear worship wars, and rightly so. This book explains that there are numerous approaches to worship, all biblically and culturally appropriate. The result is that everyone gains a new appreciation for differing styles within a context of courtesy, selflessness, and a willingness to listen to opposing views.

0-8054-3017-2

AVAILABLE AT FINE CHRISTIAN BOOKSTORES EVERYWHERE